Thank you for
visit to Bakken.

God's peace.

[signature]

Rose-Marie   August 2019
John   GOODWIN

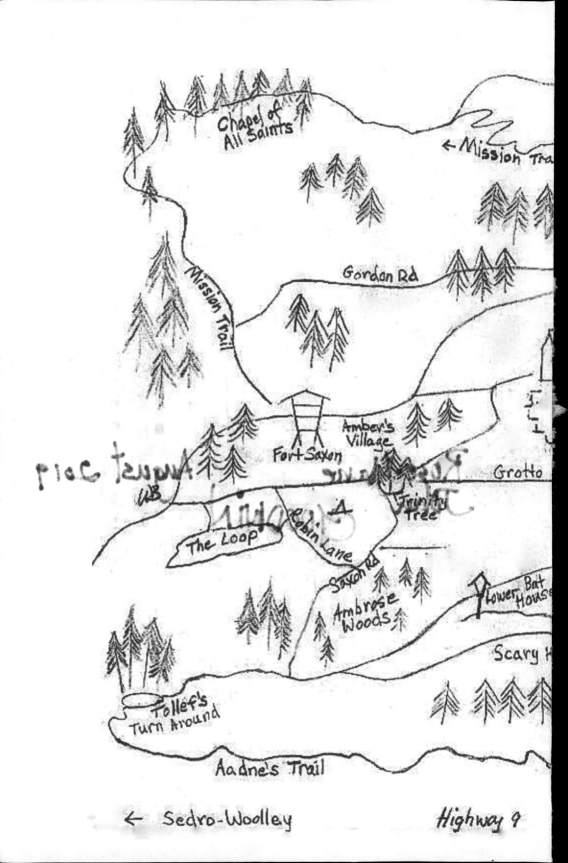

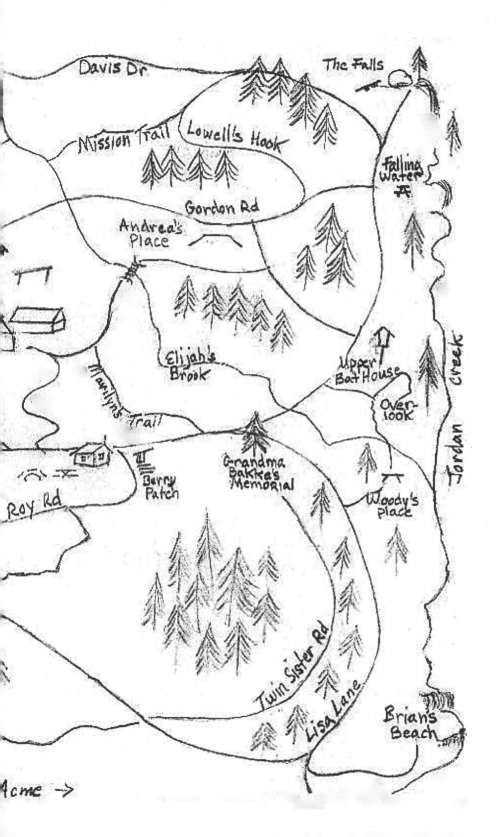

Davis Dr

The Falls

Mission Trail   Lowell's Hook

Falling Water

Gordon Rd

Andrea's Place

Elijah's Brook

Marilyn's Trail

Upper Bat House

Over-look

Jordan Creek

Grandma Bakka's Memorial

Berry Patch

Woody's Place

Roy Rd

Twin Sister Rd

Lisa Lane

Brian's Beach

Acme →

A Surprising Journey

From Saxon to Chicago and Back

Ray Bakke

Bakken Books

Acme, Washington

Illustrations by Woody Bakke
Mary of Nazareth drawing by Sam Gore
Cover design by Greg Pearson

ISBN: 978-0-9755345-1-9

Also by Ray Bakke

Lausanne Occasional Papers, No. 9: Thailand Report – Christian Witness to Large Cities

Unreached Peoples '82: The Challenge of the Church's Unfinished Business: Focus on Urban Peoples

Evangelisation i Storbyen
(Translation of lectures given in Denmark)

The Expanded Mission of 'Old First' Churches
With Samuel K. Roberts

The Urban Christian

Espoir Pour La Ville (French)
with Andre Pownall and Glenn Smith

Word in Life Study Bible
(Urban theme editor: 1200 articles)

A Theology as Big as the City

A Biblical Word for an Urban World

Street Signs: A New Direction in Urban Ministry
with Jon Sharpe

DEDICATION

Norman Kim Maleng
17 September 1938 – 24 May 2007

Norm, as he was known professionally, was Kim to those of us who grew up with him on our farms near Acme, Washington, and at Mount Baker High School, where he was valedictorian for our class of '56.

Nearly every day of our eleven years together in elementary and high school, we rode the school bus, most often in the same seat, discussing or arguing baseball, religion, and politics. We began piano lessons together in the fourth grade, and a few times performed for our classes. His Aunt Edna was our fourth grade teacher; his Aunt Ruth our sixth grade teacher and school principal. He clearly was our leader. At times we called him "Governor," because we knew he had political aspirations. He was a state champion speaker and debater. The one time he had a speaking conflict, I subbed for him when eight students from our county spent two days in Olympia with legislative leaders and Governor Langlie. We competed in the ninth grade when challenged by our English teacher, Miss Warner, to go for the school record in reading. I read and reported verbally on 278 books that year, three or four more than Kim read. But, unlike me, he also did the rest of the homework and got straight A's as usual.

At graduation we split for decades. I went to Chicago and the urban world. He finished law school, military service, and worked in a Washington, D. C. government office. Finally, he became King County Prosecuting Attorney in Seattle for twenty-eight years, until his sudden death two years ago. Whenever I visited from Chicago, I would stop by his office. When I made plans to relocate here, I asked if he would join my board and help me transition to Seattle. At his death he was chairman of our board at Bakke Graduate University.

When I returned to Washington State in 2000, I was astonished to see how he had become a virtual pastor for Seattle from the prosecutor's office, especially during the fearful twenty-year period while the murderer of forty-eight young girls remained at large. I watched him adjudicate the case into a settlement that brought justice to Gary Ridgeway, some comfort to the forty-eight families, and relief to the whole city. Taking his faith public at the press conference and replacing the Scripture from I Corinthians 13 into the official document, he articulated to the press, the city, indeed the nation and the watching world, how we must balance truth with justice in the public square.

When his daughter Karen was tragically killed in a sledding accident in 1989, in tears he called me to say he was sorry he could not make it to the Alumnus of the Year ceremony that Seattle Pacific was giving me. He told me that she would be buried up in Saxon, at the little country cemetery where our baby daughter was buried. Losing Karen was tough, but a few years later, each time I saw his wife Judy, she was being hugged by kids of color that she tutored. Then we gathered again, and laid him next to Karen on a gorgeous day in May. The nearby church filled with a mix of family, neighbors, Seattle lawyers, and high school classmates. So I say: Kim, this book is for you, and like you I truly believe that hope springs eternal. See you in the morning.

Ray

CONTENTS

FOREWORD

R ay Bakke is a missio-nomad. The world is his parish. He not only talks about a theology of place, and places – he lives it. At one point Bakken was just "the hill," an uninhabited slope facing the mountains on the opposite side of the Nooksack River Valley. In 2000 it became a peopled-place that ultimately would reflect almost 2000 years of church and mission history. Ray embodies Augustine's aphorism that he quotes in this book: "the past is a present memory . . . " In his own words: "Scratch me and you will find I bleed Luther, Augustine, Roger Williams and a host of ancient church fathers."

I first met Ray in 1982 when we brought him to speak to the Global Management Group of the Foreign Mission Board, SBC in retreat at the Glen Eyrie conference center outside Lynchburg, Virginia. After the first evening session, Ray asked me if we could drive in to Lynchburg and find the Thomas Road Baptist Church. Instant chemistry! Here is a fellow explorer, ever curious, ever daring. Returning to Eagle Eyrie after 1:00 am, I knew this was just the beginning of a long and meaningful friendship.

Subsequently, I worked with Ray in a variety of settings: Evangelicals for Middle East Understanding, his Pac Rim steering committee, and ultimately as a Regent at Bakke Graduate University. After moving to Birmingham where I assumed the role of founding director of the Global Center at Samford University, Ray came three years in succession to lead urban strategy conferences.

In all these settings Ray's passion for cities burned hot continuously and consistently. His passion is fed by both his theology and his sense of history. This book is a window into the heart and mind of Ray Bakke. If it started out as a guide to the mission trail, (which he ably accomplishes), it morphed into a combination of memoir, autobiographical reflections, and a personalized bibliography.

The themes of Ray's life are intertwined and inseparable, whether they are abstract ones like grace and Trinity, or concrete ones like trees, books, and community. All these were forged in the setting of a hard-working family where Ray learned early how to work with his hands as well as his head. Bakken mirrors this marriage as Ray gave physical shape to the symbols of missional pilgrimage across the ages.

Bakke Graduate University provides an institutional framework for contextualized learning in Asia, Africa, and Latin America. Multi-cultural training happens as students from these continents become a cohort and learn theology from the ground up together, mixing cognitive and experiential learning simultaneously. Through International Urban Associates, Ray had been facilitating networks for years within these continents as collaborative models. Now they become foundational for theological training region by region through BGU filters, giving feet to Ray's heady dreams.

Should you have the opportunity to visit Bakken and experience this microcosm of whole church, whole world imagery, you will be equally awed and inspired by all it points to: the God of creation and redemption. If you never make it to Acme, Washington, I trust you are reading this volume and realizing that God is faithful to God's own mission across the ages through resident aliens like Ray Bakke. Early on Ray determined he would not get in the trenches of historical scholarship, but to quote him, "would try to make sense of it in a world shifting from rural to urban, where the world now resided in the neighborhoods of my parishes." This missio-nomad is still on pilgrimage and has paved the way for others who share his vision to enlarge the tent and strengthen the stakes.

He has certainly helped me make more sense out of this world, and I am eternally indebted.

Bill O'Brien

INTRODUCTION

After more than forty years of wandering through cities on six continents, while using Chicago as my laboratory for thirty-five of them, Bakken is providing me the opportunity to reflect and integrate some of the key components of a spirituality that has sustained me.

Let me briefly describe how we decided to return to my boyhood mountain community up near the Canadian border, between two mythological places of my childhood: Acme to the north, and Saxon to the east. It is a critical part of a surprising journey.

In 1987, with a day off between ministry assignments in Stuttgart, Germany, a bishop's wife and son drove Corean and me three hours to Gunsbach, a village in Alsace, France. We went to visit the museum home of Dr. Albert Schweitzer, a long-time medical missionary in Africa. Albert had grown up in this village and learned to play the organ at the church where his father, a Lutheran, was the Protestant minister. After this visit, we began to ask each other where we might end up. Given permission to dream, I proposed we think about the little community of Acme, the village of my father.

Two years later we told the family, and asked my Aunt Ruth to watch for available property. Four months later, on a ministry trip to Seattle complete with a quick dash to visit some relatives, she and her daughter Sandy informed me that they had found a piece of land for us. On that rainy April evening as darkness fell, I walked up a road too steep for ordinary cars to find a partially built, but long abandoned log cabin in a small clearing. In the brush I saw a cedar tree with three trunks, and up a winding path found a waterfall. I phoned Corean that night, in Chicago, telling her the news, and asking her to send a check for one thousand dollars as earnest money. By faith, she did that. In December we built our first brush fire and planted our first trees: one hundred Douglas fir seedlings. The following summer we camped in a tent for two weeks.

My cousin, Gordon Bakke, had just returned from Africa. With a second mortgage on our one hundred year old Chicago house, I hired him for two years to work on the place between our annual visits. Roy Johnson brought his D6 Cat to remove some logs and build a car-accessible road up from the highway. On successive visits and vacation months over eight years, we completed the cabin, washhouse, pump house, marked out the mission trail, and improvised an outdoor chapel.

Bakke farm, our family homestead dating from the 1880's with the house where my father was born in 1912, lies three miles southeast, immediately across the South Fork Bridge of the Nooksack River. The Saxon Cemetery is located midway between Highway 9 and the family farm. In my youth I attended the little Lutheran church across the road from that cemetery. Sunday school was in English; preaching was in Norwegian. Dad loved taking us into the cemetery and introducing us to the friends and family we never knew, the alumni association of our little church, our "great cloud of witnesses."[1]

In the year 2000, after a decade of planning and praying, we left our Chicago inner city community where sixty thousand people lived in a one mile square, and where students from sixty-three nations could be found in our sons' high school. We came back to a valley where, for a

---

[1] Hebrews 12:1

6

little Norwegian boy to meet a Swede, was a cross-cultural experience.

I made a habit of joining the early morning coffee conversations of local loggers, truckers, and farmers at the Acme General Store, where the coffee was 25 cents, refills were free, and *The Bellingham Herald* was included. Conversations were priceless. Listening one's way into a culture is the equivalent of language school for missionaries. I had much to learn. The community had not changed physically, but the issues were different. The minorities were native, not black. Many of the struggles and prejudices were familiar.

We moved into our little one room cabin for one and a half years while Corean collaborated with Pat Mitchell, our architect, and Mark Gallatin, our builder, as our house took shape.

We searched for a name for our place, a name that people would immediate recognize as belonging to us. Bakke is Norwegian for "hill." When *n* is added to Bakke, the result – *Bakken* – means "the hill." It works. Letters addressed to Bakken are placed in the correct postbox at the Acme Post Office. However, the postmistress prefers to have Box 157 included and always reminds us with a bright red sticker.

There were seven seminaries in Vancouver, Canada. Over the years I had taught or spoken in two of them. I assumed I might be teaching in the north, so living between Seattle and Vancouver would make sense. While living in the cabin, I commuted to Seattle. What I did not know was that a new seminary, Northwest Graduate School, had opened in the Seattle area. Our future would become inextricably part of that little school.

What follows is a brief attempt to think theologically about my life, my calling, and my family, and to integrate my urban and international mission experience into our rural context.

PART I: THEMES

There are three basic ways to study the Bible. Most people use two of them regularly. They study the commands of the Bible and seek to obey them. They find principles taught in the stories and try to live by them. But there is also a third way to study the Bible. About ninety times in the prophetic books of the Old Testament, God's people are told to remember how God led in the past, and to reflect on those implications for the present.

For example:

Joseph reflected with his brothers on how their sale of him as a slave to Egypt, years earlier, resulted in his promotion to economic, social, and political leadership at a time of crisis. He told his brothers: "You meant it for evil, but God meant it for good."

Mordecai told Esther: "Perhaps this is why you were chosen to be the queen." The word *God* does not appear in the book of Esther. One theme in this book, with obvious benefit for those of us living in a secular world where God is not known or not mentioned, is the permission to look backwards and see God's leading. We cannot be dogmatic, so the word *perhaps* is a fitting way to view the past.

Jesus told many parables, the immediate meaning of which was not always obvious to his followers. With his stories, he coached them into the Biblical work of theological reflection.

Jesus spent forty days in the desert wilderness communing with God, and also identifying with the forty-year testing of the Hebrew people on their journey through the desert with Moses, more than one thousand years earlier.

Paul reminds Philemon: "Perhaps this is why Onesimus was taken from you, so you could have him back forever."

St. Augustine, the North African theologian and church leader who died in the siege of his city in AD 430, made famous this aphorism: "For the Christian, the past is a present memory, and the future is a present possibility." Put simply, a Christian lives simultaneously in three time zones: past, present and future.

As a history major back in college, I studied revolutions and learned that they have at least two benefits: first, they require that participants be informed; secondly, they force people to set priorities. When I reflect on my own journey, I see events that informed and expanded my rather narrow world-view. I also see events that challenged my Christian faith, forcing me to set priorities.

Perhaps you know that the Lutheran liturgy begins with confession. That is my reality. I know that I am a sinner and saved by the grace of God and the works of Jesus Christ on my behalf. Even though my ordination and ministry calling emerged in the Baptist church, I grew up Lutheran, and now Corean is Lutheran by choice. Scratch me and you will find I bleed Luther, Augustine, Roger Williams, and a host of ancient church fathers.

Grace emerges as a central theme in my first century mission hero, Barnabas of Cyprus. In a marvelous study on the church at Antioch, missionary evangelist E. Stanley Jones called Barnabas a "grace apostle," in contrast to Paul, a "truth apostle." Barnabas was in the rescue business and modeled it in servant roles throughout the book of Acts, especially in his reaching out and mentoring of Paul and that other flawed young missionary, John Mark.

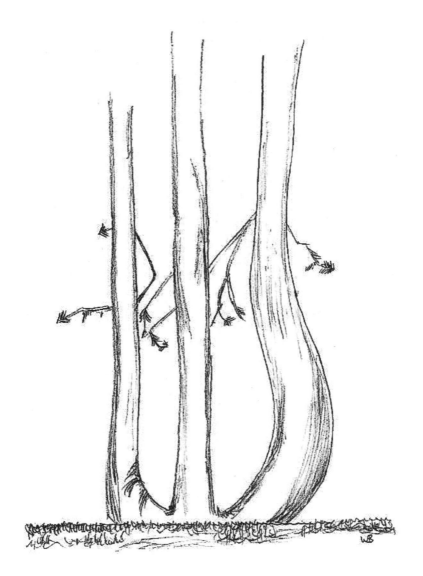

TRINITY TREE

The mission trail at Bakken begins at the Trinity Tree. It may surprise many to learn that *Trinity* is not a word used in the Bible. A North African lawyer, Tertullian, coined the word about AD 200. As a scholarly layman he had noticed that God is called Father, Son, and Holy Spirit in numerous texts. A century later, between 399 and 419, Augustine wrote *De Trinitate*, a fifteen-volume work. It has been central to the church's faith commitment, as seen in the ancient Apostles' Creed and the Nicene Creed, agreed upon by all Christian churches in the Orthodox, Catholic, and Protestant traditions since AD 325.

I will try to briefly explain some of the implications of this ancient truth.

The primary life of God is community. Augustine first described how the three persons modeled inter-penetrating relationships. Put simply, we are never more like God than when we live in community and meaningful relationships. For me this is an obvious contrast to the *lone ranger* independent life so celebrated in western and American culture, and even to those who say: I can be Christian without being part of the church.

The primary work of God is in partnerships, where each person in the Trinity has a calling and a primary vocation: Creator, Redeemer, and Sustainer of the universe, the world and everything in it. Yet we see in Genesis, John, and Ephesians that each also participates in the work of the others. These biblical descriptions of a working God help me appreciate that not only are we created to work, our work can be unique. Your calling and mine, like those of the Trinity, are equal in God-given significance. I would not dare argue that God the Creator is more important than the Redeemer or Sustainer; nor would I argue that my calling is more valued by God than yours.

My idea of the dignity and equality of the human family – father, mother, and child – corresponds to what I understand to be the equality of the heavenly family: Father, Son, and Holy Spirit. The mutual submission of each member of the Trinity to one another becomes the model for mutual submission of husbands and wives as we strive for integration in our human family relationships. I would no more argue for a hierarchy in earthly families than I would of the heavenly family.

The Trinity reminds us that God did not create humanity because God needed loving relationships. Such an idea becomes grotesque as we reflect on an eternal God so lonely that we were created to meet God's need for fellowship. Quite the contrary. God created us to share and grow in the love and relationships that exist eternally in God.

God created us to share what we receive through ministry. Knowing God, I will not be need-driven in my ministry. The needs of people shape my priorities but not my motives. I am to remember that I serve you, not because you have a need I can fulfill, but because God has done so much for me.

Suppose, as Dr. Francis Collins has suggested in *The Language of God*,[2] that God created the universe with a big bang cosmic explosion fourteen billion years ago, and that the little ball we call earth was created four billion years ago. That is no problem for me because the Bible

---

[2] NY: Free Press, 2007.

clearly begins, "In the beginning, God created the heavens and the earth." What if there is a ten billion year gap between creation of galaxies and creation of the earth? What is that to an eternal God? The Hebrew word translated "in the beginning" is a timeless participle.

What *does* give me pause is Paul's idea in Ephesians that we were chosen by God to be redeemed, even before the foundations of the earth were created. For some Christians, it must seem like a colossal waste of time that God spent so much time creating things instead of speedily focusing on saving souls. How does this shape my own view of mission and urgency? I confess now to having some difficulty with those who keep saying: "Just preach the gospel," or, "Just do evangelism." Is not this a kind of functional unitarianism, when a person cares about the agendas of only one member of the Trinity, in this case, Jesus?

The Trinity expands my idea of mission. God is redeeming the human race, and all of creation that has been spoiled by sin, beginning with personal and extending to massive systems of evil. The garden God created has become a dangerous reality to many people, places, and species of a potentially exquisite planet.

I have been told that this mountain was logged around 1920. A few old growth fir trees appear to have been cut down and then abandoned, perhaps because they cracked or broke as they fell. God created the mountain and seems to have used the ice age to sculpt it in many remarkable ways. I counted approximately one thousand trees on these twelve acres when we purchased in 1992. I have planted more than two thousand trees since we arrived here in 2000.

We harvested maple trees to cover the costs of running power and phone lines into Bakken. After clearing out a lot of brush, we now plant and nurture a new generation of fir, cedar, and alder, interspersed with walking trails and tractor roads named for family members and neighbors who encouraged us on the journey. For me, the trails have become a prayer walk where work and worship visibly integrate.

I learned from my studies with Orthodox scholars that the Holy Spirit works in cultures before missionaries get there. That understanding impacted the way I approached cities over the decades of my own ministry. I go to cities, not to observe terrible conditions or desperate needs so often in the headlines, but to look for signs of hope. I want to begin by discovering what the Spirit has been teaching the people and the churches before I present plans for change.

I began ministry in Seattle as a youth and music minister in 1959. A year earlier, Martin Luther King led the civil rights marches. I was forced to confront my own cultural history and the white privileges that had benefited me along the way. Knowing God had called me to city ministry, I knew early on that I would usually be in a white minority, working primarily in black or Hispanic communities outside my traditional comfort zone.

Boeing lost a huge contract from the Pentagon, to design and build airplanes in Seattle. That contract was withdrawn as part of a political deal between Lyndon Johnson and John Kennedy in the 1960 election. Almost overnight my congregation in Seattle became unemployed by the decision to shift government money from Seattle to southern-based airplane manufacturers. I understood then that cities were not random collections of people. Cities often package people into economic systems. I made a vow to understand cities. That prodded me to return to Chicago for further studies.

Our third child died only hours before her birth in 1965, as a result of German measles that Corean caught during the first week of pregnancy. For nine months we waited for the outcome of a "war in the womb." If she lived, she could be blind and could have heart and brain damage. Since I was about to finish college at Seattle Pacific, it would have meant working locally to support what we assumed would be an institutionalized child. We had no insurance. The baby we had planned to name Robin gave her life for us. We buried her in the Saxon Cemetery alongside other family members in this very special place.

At the graveside service I announced to our family and friends that we would be moving to Chicago. Like the man born blind, I was asking: How will I ever see the glory of God in the death of our baby?

No sooner had we moved to Chicago and into the inner city, at great expense and considerable difficulty, than I lit a match to a faulty stove, putting myself into the local hospital emergency room. I had burns on my arms, hands, and face. Skin hung like black moss off my arms. It was close to midnight when my two doctors finished cutting and bandaging. On my left was a Chinese refugee doctor who told me she fled China to North Korea, then to South Korea, and finally to Chicago, the promised land. My surgeon on the right had owned two hospitals in Cuba, but gave them to Castro for five plane tickets so he could bring his family to Chicago and to freedom.

I had assumed I would be coming to the city to study and perhaps also minister among the urban migrants and refugees I had read or heard about. I did not expect that God would provide two doctors, both exiles from communist countries, who would minister to me. I made a vow that if and when I got out of the hospital, I would study how God uses refugees in world evangelization. From Abraham to the present, refugees who see themselves as victims may be integral to God's mission in the transformation of the church and the liberation of the whole world.

The flight of the evangelical white churches from the cities to the suburbs in the 1960's rocked my world. Darwin, Marx, and Freud had been a tough mental challenge in seminars at the University of Washington years earlier, but nothing in my theology had prepared me for the obvious racism I experienced in my church and denomination by 1965. Mentors at the Moody Bible Institute and Trinity

20

Evangelical Divinity School never exposed me to biblical ideas of the city. One day in January 1966, I was reading an essay by urban sociologist Steven Rose. He asserted that conservative Christians could not survive in cities. For him, the Bible is a rural book. God's favorite people, like David, are shepherds. God makes gardens. His least favorite people are urban dwellers.

About this time I was watching churches evacuate cities all across the country, especially in New York, Detroit, Newark, Chicago, Los Angeles, and where major riots were happening. More shocking to me was the idea that the Christians who fled all claimed to have "correct" views of the Bible, missions, and Holy Spirit.

Like I suggested earlier, a good challenge forces one to become informed and to set priorities. Again I made vows. I would study Chicago, a place I did not know, that I might learn to love my new city. And I would study the Bible to see if there was a theology as big as the city. My searches became titles of books I wrote later. My contagious love for Chicago and city churches is the story told in *The Urban Christian*. My search of urban themes in the Bible resulted in *A Theology as Big as The City*. Both books were published by InterVarsity Press and have been translated into other languages.

Five years before we moved to Bakken in 2000, I designed a two thousand foot mission trail that, together with grotto and chapel, reminds me of the "great cloud of witnesses" that crossed all boundaries of this world to pass on the good news of the Gospel of our Lord Jesus Christ. They passed the torch. It is our turn now.

I believe that the Holy Spirit has given gifts of many kinds in every generation. For me to ignore that is to neglect God's teaching given to the church since Pentecost. I call myself a historical charismatic because I look for God's creative and redemptive work in the history of the world. For me, the world has become the playing field of the Spirit, so to ignore any time or place willfully represents a denial of God's teaching for today. To truly know and reflect on historical and missional theology becomes yet one more way to love God with our minds.

As you walk around Bakken, you will see trails and places named for a few of the people who have profoundly changed my life. I often think of how my dad or Uncle Aadne would have loved to share this mountain experience with us. Dad died in 1990 just months before he had hoped to relocate from eighteen years in Colorado to his beloved Washington. I named one trail *Tollef's Trail* because it heads south and east toward Saxon and the Bakke family homestead and farm where he grew up, about three miles from here. This trail stops abruptly with a tractor turn around, reminding me that Dad never made it back. A walking trail, named for his younger brother Aadne, follows the curving hillside along the east side of the property, about one hundred feet above the highway.

The little raspberry and blueberry patch – with the old outhouse – near the log cabin has a sign reading *Ruth's Place*. Mom supervised berry pickers on many farms. In 1992 when we came to camp in a tent, I went to one of those farms and asked for an old outhouse. They told me to pick one. Corean cleans it regularly and it gets used. It was the first building on this property.

Along the various trails you may hear or see *Jordan Creek*, which I named for our first grandson on his thirteenth birthday. On the official map it was called *No Name Creek*. At a time when *Dawson's Creek* was a popular television program, I decided Jordan could have a creek.

The brook is named for Elijah, who came later. Amber has her village, a children's play area. The map of Bakken has become complex with special places, trails, and roads

25

named for our sons and daughters-in-law as well. *Roy's Road* is named for my long time Sunday school teacher, Roy Johnson. The first road we made to the cabin, *Aunt Ruth Road*, is named in honor of the realtor who found this property for us, my Aunt Ruth. These names remind me that we do not own, but steward this land.

One tractor road is named *Robin* for the stillborn daughter who gave her life for us. Next to it, a road named *The Loop* reminds me that, following her burial, we moved to Chicago. In the center of the city there is a mile-by-mile square ringed by elevated tracks and trains, known as the Loop.

At the driving entrance to our property there is a special grove of trees we named *The Triangle*, where I attempted to plant a tree from various geographical locations of the Bakke family. Along with a cedar of Lebanon that reminds me of Bible lands, at the center I planted an African cedar from the Atlas Mountains of North Africa. I wanted it to represent the Africans in our extended family, and also the mission work of Gordon and his family, who spent twenty-four years of their lives in Zambia. The idea was to let the Africans and the African Americans in our family – we have both – know that they are at the center and not at the fringe. What they have taught and brought to us over the years has shaped us in amazing ways. We celebrate their presence with us. Unfortunately, as of this writing, the African cedar, now nine years old, may not survive this climate.

26

The Bakke family helped shape, but also remains forever imprinted by the special ethos of Saxon and the Nooksack River Valley, a place beneath the Twin Sister Mountains and Mount Baker. I grew up on the eastern side of the valley, a location largely without direct sun for the dreary months of fall, winter, and spring. The place Aunt Ruth found for us is on the west side of Stewart Mountain, which rises thirty-five hundred feet above our house. It is a much larger mountain than it looks, as I can attest after spending five hours climbing to the top, mostly through brush and logged areas as I sought the source of our creek. That hike was a gift to myself on my sixty-ninth birthday.

Across the valley, Saxon Hill rises twenty-five hundred feet above sea level. In my high school years I was all over that mountain, looking for cedar slabs left by loggers, from which I could cut shake blanks and sell for roof shingles. I had a little business in those years, run with equipment I gradually bought from my earnings picking strawberries. As an eighth grader, I bought a tractor – a 1938 hand crank Farmall F 12 high wheel tractor – from a classmate, Ray Hockett, with four hundred dollars of my own money. At sixteen I acquired a 1938 Dodge pickup, and with Ed Maleng's help I installed a 1948 Dodge engine, purchased for one hundred dollars from another neighbor. I was able to use my dad's Homelight power saw because he was in Alaska and not using it. One summer I hired Eddie for one dollar per hour. We cut and sold many truck loads of shake blanks, but most of that money was needed to repair the truck, the saw, and buy more used tires to replace frequent flat tires.

Work was hard and hours were long, between milking on our family farm, making hay, and picking berries six days a week. In my library you can see a picture of what I looked like at age seventeen in the summer before my senior year, as I worked alongside Pat Mitchell, then sixteen. Pat went off to school later to become an architect. I had the privilege of baptizing him while I was interim pastor of Elim Baptist Church in Seattle, and also performing his wedding to Marilyn. What we did not know then, was that forty years later he would work with us to design our house.

Bakken is across the highway and up a hill from the Maleng farm where my boyhood schoolmates, Henry and Kim Maleng grew up, and where Henry and his wife Vivian live today.

During the spring of our fourth grade year, an over-wide log truck, coming north on Highway 9, rounded the curve where Old Stone Way now joins the highway, and hit our school bus going south. A log sheared off part of the bus. Ambulances arrived from two counties and took sixteen people to hospitals. Kim and I were sitting together at the back of the bus. Like most the others, we clambered out the emergency door and fled to the nearby creek to wash blood off our faces and glass out of our hair. We found out later that Jane Westra, who had just moved into the district, died in the arms of our seriously wounded bus driver, Bessie Ambrose. Our fourth grade teacher, Edna Maleng, had been sitting in the first row and was also among the seriously injured.

The highway has been considerably widened and straightened in recent years. I often pause at the bottom of the hill, before turning onto the highway, and remember that experience. Why Jane and not me, I ask?

Ruth Anderson was our sixth grade teacher and the principal of Acme grade school for the years I was there.[3] She was a terrific teacher and had a voice that you could not avoid hearing from great distances, especially if you had crossed her in some way. Malengs, Andersons, and other neighbors as well as Bakke relatives lived all around us. When we misbehaved, there was no place to hide. My mom always knew what I had done wrong before I got home from school. The village helped raise every kid in my generation.

I grew up by the Nooksack River, near the original Bakke homestead. We did not have indoor plumbing until Dad installed it when I was in the sixth grade. I spent lots of cold morning and evening times in our outhouse, often reading old Sears or Wards catalogues, which sometimes doubled as toilet paper.

Our house went down the Nooksack River in the great flood of 1955, my senior year in high school and the very day of my final football game at Mt Baker. I had gone to school that day as usual. After lunch I heard a message on the school intercom. My sister and I were to immediately leave for home, picking up our younger brothers from school in Acme on the way.

When we arrived, we found many cars and trucks and people who had come to help. Marilyn's bedroom and the living room had already fallen into the river. Loggers

---

[3] Editor's note: Since living in Acme as a newcomer to the community, I have been told that the name is Acme Elementary School. A sign over the entrance reads Acme Consolidated School. Ray always called it Acme grade school and so it shall be in this book, with non-capitalized letters for the ambiguous portions of the name.

were carrying furniture from the remaining house into a U-haul truck.

With Dad in a remote location in Alaska and totally out of touch, Mom took charge, giving orders to people known and unknown. She called WVOS, the local radio station in Bellingham, and instructed them to announce that anyone knowing of an available house should contact the station. She also called the sheriff's office with instructions for when a house would be found, including the officers in her ever-widening circle of helpers.

She told me to take Lowell, Dennis, and Marilyn with me in the truck now filled with our furniture, and start driving toward Bellingham. I should not worry about where I was going because a policeman would stop me, and guide us to our destination. I was stopped in Deming where we drove to an abandoned, rickety house with no interior doors. While I played my final football game, Mom cleaned and decorated so we could have a party that very night after the game. When we went to bed that night, the blankets Mom had hung for temporary doors fluttered in the breeze. Dad arrived from Alaska two weeks later, astonished that we now lived in Deming.

About twenty-five years after the flood, I lectured a sophisticated graduate school audience in a Boston theological seminary. I had been asked by its president to speak about pastoring in the midst of the violent inner city Chicago community where I had served for a decade. Two professors of psychology and counseling waited until everyone else had gone and then they said, "You don't get it do you?" Surprised, and not knowing what to say, I think I asked what it was I didn't get. More surprising was their next question. "You got a lot of love when you were a kid, didn't you?" "Well, yes," I remember saying, but I also told them I had rural, second-generation peasant roots.

30

What I did not get became clearer after their explanation: "You seem to believe that these graduate students could do what you did in a mixed racial inner city neighborhood, if only they had the right information and motivation for their ministries."

They went on to remind me that being rural and being poor was not the point. I had gotten a lot of love as a kid in a family and in a community, and unlike nearly everyone in my audience that day, I had been born into an identity I did not earn.

I was identified by family and by geography, by being Tollef and Ruth's kid, and being from the Bakke farm. Unlike today's sophisticated students, I could afford to take risks and make downward mobility an art form. It did not matter if my church succeeded or failed. My calling was deeply rooted. I did not require professional ordination or a successful church to know I was a good pastor. They reminded me that information and motivation alone does not predict success for people who lack strong relational affirmation.

They spoke truth. When you ask rural kids who they are, they tell you who they are by pointing to their family and geography. When you ask city people who they are, they respond differently. They tell you what they do. They usually say, I'm a teacher, or, I work at Boeing. That was a great learning moment for me. Urban unemployment is far more disastrous than rural unemployment. If you lose your job, as Dad did often while we were kids, it is an economic problem for sure. But when urban adults lose their jobs, it is also an identity crisis.

Bakkes and Malengs and our high achieving cousins and neighbors, along with many others we knew, are not the self-made heroic types some people think. We are not people who studied and achieved by information and motivation alone, often without the benefit of premier education institutions. We were people who were loved by schoolteachers, Sunday school friends, band directors, and coaches, but above all by neighbors in a community that cared for kids. We were loved, and with that security, we could take risks. Bakken is a place for remembering our community.

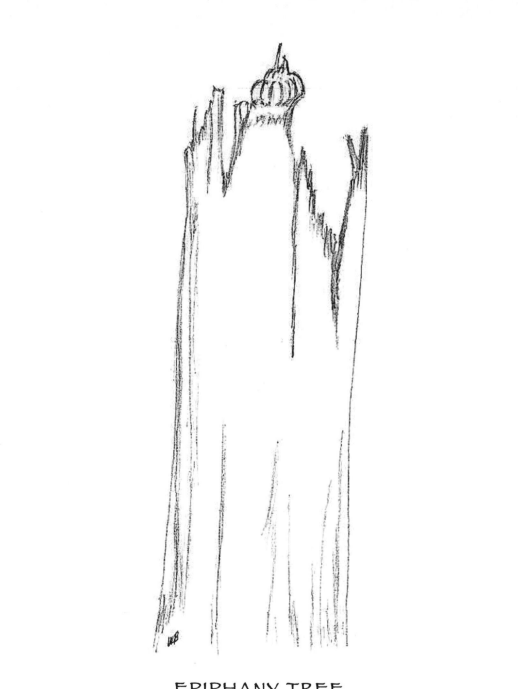

EPIPHANY TREE

When you look out of the east windows of our house, you will see a huge cedar snag – a broken battered old tree still standing – perhaps more than six hundred years old, which makes it older than the Protestant Reformation and the theological tradition I am identified with. The architect made that snag the "point on line" for the house that faces directly east.

Look more closely at the top and you may notice an onion shaped dome. That dome formation reminds me of the ancient Orthodox churches of the east. I call this our Epiphany Tree. Epiphany is that special season after Christmas when we remember the star that appeared over Bethlehem and drew the "Wise Men," worshipers probably from far off Babylon. They were non-Jews, so let Epiphany represent a breakthrough in the Bible, when people saw with fresh insight what God was doing in the world, and responded in worship. The Gospel came to us from the east. For me, this tree represents the eastern churches

Since 1976 I have made repeated trips to the Middle East, and have friends in many of the ancient Orthodox churches. Much of my theology came from the Cappadocian Fathers and from Antioch, Alexandria, other parts of North Africa, the Gulf areas, and from Rome. At least seventy percent of what Luther, Calvin, and Wesley taught us was drawn from those ancient theological wells from which they drank deeply. Whenever leaders re-visit these ancient sources, renewal comes to the church. That is happening all over God's earth. The Kingdom of God is multi-generational.

An Armenian Orthodox Bishop once reminded a small audience of us in Cyprus that when Christians in the west think of the great commission and missions in the Bible, they usually think of going horizontally to the nations in one generation. By way of contrast, the Orthodox leaders usually did not have the privilege of travel because they lived under political oppression for most of their history. They think of the great commission in vertical terms. Will they faithfully transmit the two thousand year old Gospel to their children in the next generation? Personally, I think their vertical faithfulness more than complements my two thousand miles of horizontal mission travel in one generation. We need each other.

I found another old snag near the 18th stake on the mission trail, removed it in sections with the help of my neighbor Rick Harkness, and installed it at the entrance door of our house. By counting rings and estimating it at about five hundred years old, I have concluded it was living when Luther and Michelangelo were alive and ministering in the sixteenth century in Germany and Italy. I call this my Reformation Tree, and put a light in it at night. It evokes Moses' burning bush, where God spoke truth long ago.

My own ordination is in the Baptist tradition, which I embraced after studying the seven volumes of Roger Williams before I finished college in 1965.[4] Back in 1639 Williams, a Puritan, relocated from Salem to found a new colony called Providence in Rhode Island. He refused to accept the ideas of John Cotton, and other Boston Puritans, that the English settlers were the new Israel, and that the local Indian tribes were Canaanites to be driven out of the land. Williams said that you cannot read the Bible that way. He became the first person to espouse the idea that

---

[4] Perry Miller, editor, *The Complete Writings of Roger Williams* (NY: Russell & Russell, 1964).

governments should not control religion or churches. It seemed so radical at the time.

Williams' views of justice and baptism issues convinced me that I could be a pastor with integrity and also pursue the pressing social issues of my era.[5] Eventually, that meant co-founding (1986) and chairing the board for Evangelicals for Middle East Understanding, working for peace, justice for all of Abraham's children: Jews, Christians, and Muslims. Arab Christians, especially Palestinian Christians, who have been so ignored and damaged by American policies and actions in the Middle East are given special advocacy by EMEU.

Williams' idea of the church was equally radical. He accepted Luther's once startling idea that all Christians are priests, responsible to God, and ought to be ministers in their vocations. Williams was the first known American to claim that adult baptism of believing Christians was ordination to ministry. He turned the hierarchy of Catholic, Lutheran, Reformed, and Anglican churches upside down. According to Williams, to baptize is to ordain.

When I was baptized I became a minister. When I was officially ordained a pastor, I gave up authority in the church and received responsibility in the church. As a Baptist pastor, I worked under the church and not over it. The church called me, paid me, and kept me accountable. In return I equipped, taught, counseled, and encouraged

---

[5] Other writings by Williams which influenced my thinking include: Roger Williams, *Key Into the Language of America* and *The Bloody Tenent of Persecution for the Cause of Conscience* (published in London, 1644); and Perry Miller, *Roger Williams: His Contribution to the American Tradition* (NY: Atheneum, 1962).

them to do the ministry. When I studied God's election and ordination of Israel in the Bible, I found that the nation's ordination was not to status, but to service. They assumed that their "chosenness" meant God's "favoriteness." Generations of prophets, many texts of Scripture, and Jesus himself persistently confronted that misunderstanding.

It was not long before I realized that this view of my ministry ordination was also a reason why I never had a problem with women in pastoral ministry. Pastoral ministry is not an authority issue but a servant calling. The only way you can keep women from ministry is to not baptize them, which seems contrary to the clear teaching of Jesus. By ordination I simply mean that what everybody may do, somebody must do. I borrowed that line from a now departed Lutheran scholar Joseph Sittler, who made that comment in a seminary symposium on ordination, at Lutheran School of Theology in Chicago more than forty years ago.

I also affirm that even though the words for church occur more than one hundred times in the New Testament, the local church is not the final goal of ministry. Local churches are to be "signs of" and "agents for" the Kingdom of God, which is a larger biblical idea than the local churches we know and love. Christ inaugurated the Kingdom in his ministry. Churches are the primary agents to achieve Kingdom agendas and values that propel our mission throughout the world until Jesus comes again and completes the work.

Sometimes I remind people that Billy and Ruth Graham were never members of the same local church. Ruth even refused to join Billy's Western Springs Baptist Church near Chicago, where he pastored after his graduation from Wheaton College. Ruth, a life long Presbyterian and baptized as a baby, simply refused to be re-baptized, the requirement to join his church. I wish they had talked more about that. It could have helped many of us today, who find that, like restaurants, no one type of food – physical or spiritual – meets the needs of diverse families, especially in the pluralistic western cultures of Europe and North America.

Corean grew up with a Mennonite father and Presbyterian mother, faithfully endured twenty years as a Baptist in my churches, and is now a Lutheran by choice. Her Mennonite simple life and peace traditions strongly influence Bakken, as many visitors have observed, especially after experiencing the house décor and meals.

By contrast, as an un-baptized child of Lutheran parents – because we moved to Alaska when I was a baby – I chose "believers' baptism" in my teenage years. Tongue in cheek, I sometimes, perhaps irreverently, say that Baptists provided real water at my baptism, and Lutherans provide me real wine at communion, and so I combine the best of both traditions. But, on the journey, both of us admit that in many ways we are closet Orthodox.

BOOKS

It was the Scottish man of letters, Walter Scott, who may have first said, "For a Christian, one book is enough, but a thousand are not too many." At a fundamental level, Bakken exists to prove that God has given us *two* very special books: the book of God's words, the Bible; and the book of God's works, creation. I have long assumed that whenever these books appear to contradict each other, I must suspend judgment until I learn more about one book or the other.

Acme grade school, about two miles north, was built the year before I was born, 1937. My love for books grew there, but only in ways a few of us knew about. In those days, at the west end of the hall between grades one and two, there was a small bookroom, stale and dusty. It had shelves on the left side, mops and brooms on the right side, and a window straight ahead.

The first day I came as a transfer student from Bellingham, I did something that upset my second grade teacher, Miss Sperber. She gave me a shaking up, which removed most of my shirt buttons, and sent me to the bookroom. I do not remember crying. Instead, I noticed lots of old books on the shelves. For some reason my teacher thought I was too bad to be kept in class, so during that year I spent many hours in the bookroom. By the third grade, I had made misbehaving an art form. As I continued reading those old discarded history books, my window on the outside world opened wide.

My fourth grade teacher, Edna Maleng, realized what was happening. She changed the punishment. Instead of going to the bookroom and reading, I remained indoors during

41

recess to do extra arithmetic. My behavior quickly changed. When I asked whether I could have those old history books, she said she would ask the principal. The next day I carried them home in a couple of paper bags. Between my fourth and fifth grade years I memorized a time line from Alexander the Great (c. 330 BC) to the present. By fifth grade I was Mr. History in the class, while other students identified with math, science, geography, and art. Class contests involved seeing if anyone could stump us with questions. Pick any year, between Alexander and 1950, and I could tell you something that occurred. I cannot explain why such things happen, but in those days before television, a rural kid took flight.

Today, there are nearly ten thousand catalogued books in my library. I remind anyone who asks, that my love for books began when teachers – whether appropriately or not can be debated – disciplined me. My voracious reading did not translate into productive study habits and good grades, as it did for Kim Maleng, our class valedictorian, but years later, as a freshman at Mt. Baker High School, I set a new record in the reading contest.

The brilliant sixteenth century renaissance scholar, Erasmus of Rotterdam, once quipped that his patron saint was the thief on the cross. When asked why, he explained: That poor thief proves that ultimately one need not know much to make it to heaven. Jesus promised the dying thief who had a repentant spirit a place in paradise that very day. By way of contrast, I also value the perspective of a great eighteenth century Christian scholar, Jonathan Edwards, who wrote a classic, *Religious Affections*,[6] to remind us that it is God's ultimate purpose to turn all our

---

[6] Jonathan Edwards, *Religious Affections*, ed. John E. Smith (New Haven CT: Yale University Press, 1959).

42

knowledge into genuine affection for God and for
Kingdom agendas.

Corean is a more disciplined reader, and an exacting
writer. The latest surprise is that she is writing and
composing and now, with our daughter-in-law, Andrea,
has started a little publishing company. Bakken Books
was begun to publish books that, like this one, might not
be of interest to any other publisher.

TREES

"Blessed is the man . . . he shall be like a tree," begins the first Psalm. Dad had lots of jobs, but for most of his life he was a logger, and so was I before going off to Bible school at age eighteen. We have tried to honor trees at Bukkon. The house is held up by seven vertical logs, about the size of the trees growing outside. I chose a gray stain for our house, to blend with the bark color of cedars and hemlock all around. A logging chain at the shed roof entrance serves as a downspout. The interior incorporates three different woods: maple on the floors and shelves, fir on doors and window trim, cedar on the ceiling. Those same kinds of trees grow around the house.

My late uncle, Henry Torkelson, gave me some beautiful trees that I planted around these twelve acres. Hundreds of young fir trees have come as gifts to me from Joyce and Lawrence Ambrose of Wickersham. David Syre gave me alder seedlings with instructions to plant them between fir trees so that both will compete for light, and grow faster and straighter. I do not need more cedars or hemlocks. Those trees grow here already and I transplant many every year.

The annual log show in this county brings thousands of people to view reenactments of skills from the economy and culture of a hundred years ago or less, when steam trains ran all over these mountains. In this politically correct era, one well-known logger told me, "I build stumps."

Trees serve many wonderful purposes. We are delighted to live among them and watch them grow. But we are also

45

realists and stewards of a mountain that, like the farms below us, works best when cultivated responsibly over the generations. My childhood house washed down the river due to the clear-cut logging done in former generations, when loggers often "raped the mountains" with the slash and burn approach right down into the creek beds. When the rains came, nothing was left to hold the soil. It slid down the mountains and filled up the rivers that now widen and whip lash through the valleys, destroying people and places.

Nearby our family farm at Saxon, there is a native managed fish hatchery we love to visit and show friends. Two million salmon are hatched there every year, and after a season of feeding in ponds, they are sent down rivers to the ocean and to the Arctic ice flows of Alaska. Those not caught return three or four years later, many to the very place where they were spawned. Long before Boeing, Microsoft, Starbucks, and Amazon – the four big economies of this state today – existed, Washington State had the 3 F's: fishing, farming and forest products.

They need each other as much as we need them on this warming and polluting planet. We know now that certain fertilizers on fields, while increasing yields for farmers, destroy fish when the rains push those alien compounds into rivers. Unlimited logging damages both fishing and farming. In legislatures and other policy bodies at county and state levels, we have a robust conversation going these days. An ecological balance is critical. The mandate to work at it comes from our first parents, Adam and Eve, who were placed in a garden and told to steward it. They started well, but failed. That mandate was never withdrawn. It has been made more difficult by the greed and sinfulness of our common humanity. Bakken is the latest opportunity my family has had to wrestle with one of the greatest challenges facing people on six continents.

46

We are not hiding in a private space for us and for our family alone. We are stewards.

Our life together here is a bit like a musical score, like a fugue with theme and variations. We have struggled often in our forty-nine years of marriage, and travels have kept us apart for weeks at a time. We light candles at meals as a reminder that life is filled with recurring motifs of work and joy, struggle and hope.

Isaac, the Hebrew patriarch, is known perhaps less for what he himself accomplished than for the fact that he had a famous father, Abraham, and an equally famous (or infamous) son, Jacob. Isaac re-dug his father's old wells – wells that I suspect had either caved in, or were simply forgotten. As I reflect theologically on my life these days, I am reminded that little of what I say or value is new. This is not mere nostalgia. It was Jaroslav Pelikan, long-time church historian at Yale, and a Lutheran who converted to Orthodoxy just before his death, who said, "Tradition is the living faith of the dead. Traditionalism is the dead faith of the living."[7]

Rural environments are more like cities today than ever before. Values and life-styles of cities have spread into the hinterlands via television. Acme is now connected to the Internet. Most of the local jobs evaporated years ago. People now commute to cities near and far to find employment. The truth is, for those of us in this valley, Vancouver is moving south toward us as fast as Seattle is moving north toward us. Just about any problem we had

---

[7] I heard this now-famous quote in person from Pelikan, and have read it in multiple books and journals.

in cities years ago, exists today on nearby native reservations. Everywhere, local and regional jails are over-crowded. After nearly a decade of listening to the complaints of farmers and loggers around the coffee table at the Acme General Store, I sense they are feeling as marginalized as many of my inner city neighbors were, and with good reason. Change has come to rural America.

The ancient philosopher Heraclites made famous an axiom: "You can't step into the same river twice." What he meant was, the river moves on and when you step in a second time, it is not the same water. But I think he also may have been reminding me that when that second time arrives, I will not be the same person as before.

For the past forty years, I studied Chicago and other major cities of the world with populations of a million or more. Now, with a changed perspective, I returned to this remote valley. As my mother used to say, "This is not the end of the world, but you can see it from here."

MARY OF NAZARETH

THE GOSPEL

As we leave the Trinity Tree and walk toward the start of the mission trail near the front of the log cabin, we will enter the Mary of Nazareth Grotto. In it we ponder a sculpture of Mary the mother of Jesus – Mary the refugee – carrying her Asian baby born in Palestine, to Egypt in North Africa. The Christmas story in Matthew reminds us that Jesus was born during the Roman occupation of Palestine. He soon became an international political refugee. All baby boys of Bethlehem, two and under, died for Jesus before he could die for them on the Cross. If anybody can appreciate the devastating impact of crack cocaine addicted babies, HIV infected babies, or alcohol impacted babies, Jesus would understand their pain. He fled, lived as an undocumented alien in a foreign country, returned, was crucified and then buried in a borrowed grave. It certainly would seem that he understands the plight of the homeless in every city today. I did not invent this story. I simply took the stained glass off the verses in Matthew, allowing us to see why I think the birth story is such good news.

Dr. Sam Gore, founder and long time professor of the art department at Mississippi College in Clinton, Mississippi, stayed in our Chicago home for a couple weeks each summer for six years, teaching in our son Brian's art camps. Sam agreed to do this sculpture and used a young Lebanese girl named Hannah as the model for Mary's Middle Eastern face. We installed it in 2000, shortly after moving here, as our fortieth anniversary remembrance. Sam later returned to Bakken for a vesper service, where, in forty-one and a half minutes, he modeled three interlocking ethic faces from a single block of red

Mississippi clay. Most recently, Sam made a drawing of Mary carrying her child for inclusion here. He is eighty-one as this book goes to press, and continues to teach and sculpt.

It surprises many when I remind them that the earliest Christians did not observe the birth of Jesus. No one in the book of Acts even mentioned it. Paul wrote letters to churches all over the Roman Empire, but never told them to remember Jesus' birth. He makes one reflective comment in Galatians: "But when the fullness of the time was come, God sent forth His Son."[8] Maybe it was hard to talk about the virgin birth with Mary sitting in the front row, but surely that cannot be the only reason.

Most scholars agree that the earliest Christians were so taken with Easter they had no need for Christmas. The Jesus they saw brutally crucified and died was buried but emerged from that tomb alive again, three days later. The disciples had forty days to meet and re-orient their whole lives around the overwhelming implications of Jesus' resurrection. When the Holy Spirit touched the one hundred twenty followers in the upper room in Jerusalem on Pentecost Sunday, fifty days after the resurrection, they were empowered and ready to share this good news. The message spread even faster when persecution forced them to leave Jerusalem on a mission that crossed boundaries of every kind. Perhaps it was thirty to forty years later before the Holy Spirit woke up Matthew and Luke, reminding them that something was missing. A fully divine, heavenly, mystical, resurrected Jesus who ascended to heaven, was only part of the story.

There were other religious options in the Roman Empire in the first century, including Gnosticism, which loved the

---

[8] Galatians 4:4

54

idea of a spirituality rooted in a heavenly Jesus with whom we can have mystical relationships. If that sounds familiar, it is. Those ideas never completely disappeared. What Gnosticism found embarrassing, perhaps even disgusting, was the idea of a God who willingly chose to intervene in history, who took on a human physical body, who grew, taught, and willingly died that awful death on the cross as the sin-bearer for anyone on earth who was willing to repent of their sin and follow him.

Over several decades I have made a serious study of the infancy narratives, the birth stories of Matthew and Luke. Like others, I have noticed that both Matthew and Luke start with cemetery tours: Matthew, a Jew, summarized the history of Jesus' ancestry back to Abraham; Luke, a Gentile, summarized history going all the way back to Adam so it could include a Greek like him. For Luke, Jesus' birth is located in time and space with implications for Augustus Caesar and the Empire itself. I searched the history to see which church fathers have spoken on these chapters. Jerome is the first I found, writing in the fourth century. He lived for twenty-five years in a cave near the Bethlehem manger and explored the sites of many biblical stories. He translated the Bible into Latin, a translation read for centuries.

I have concluded that researching and remembering the stories of Jesus' birth, when they were possibly nearly forgotten, represents a theological revolution in the mission message of the early church, one we need to recover and boldly proclaim today. Why does Matthew's good news begin with that list of dead people, with what I call a cemetery tour? And why does Matthew mention the four women – Tamar, Rahab, Ruth, and Mrs. Uriah whom we know as Bathsheba – in the opening paragraph of his good news? Are not those Old Testament stories the "R

Rated" ones we do not mention in pulpits or polite company?

Luther was the first to observe in print that all four women were foreigners. Perhaps Stephen Neill was right also, when he said there is a mission parenthesis around Matthew's gospel. Chapter twenty-eight tells us to go, witness, and disciple the ethnic groups. Chapter one reminds us to not forget the scandalous Canaanites, Moabites, and Hittites, those despised peoples that existed alongside ancient Jews of Israel, often persecuting them.

Perhaps the late Catholic scholar, Raymond Brown was also right with his idea that Matthew may have been doing some Bible study and creating a support group for Mary and thinking something like this: "Mary, you are not the only woman in the Bible who has trouble explaining where your kid came from. Here are four soul friends who had the same problem." I can neither prove nor disprove that idea, but I like the pastoral care for Mary implied in that suggestion.[9]

Matthew, writing in the context of Gnosticism that swirled around some of the first century communities, chose to remind us that Jesus – the only person in history free to choose the DNA on his human side – deliberately choreographed scandalous racial groups into his blood lineage: the cursed race of Canaan after Noah's flood; the incestuous race of Moab which emerges from Lot and the Sodom story; and the warlike culture of Hittites which included Uriah and his wife. All four of these grandmothers of Christmas contrast with Mary, the young mother of Jesus.

---

[9] Raymond Brown, *The Birth of the Messiah: A Commentary on the Infancy Narratives in Matthew and Luke* (Garden City NY: Doubleday, 1977).

Matthew, as well as Luke, teaches that on the divine side, Jesus was virgin born, the sinless Son of God. And Matthew also teaches that on the human side, Jesus had mixed blood from other people groups. Some are quick to remind me that Matthew records Joseph's blood line, not Mary's. Luke records Mary's. Therefore Joseph's ancestry would not impact Jesus.

I have only one problem with that. My study of the other genealogies of the Old Testament, such as Exodus 6 and the first nine chapters I Chronicles, reminds me that the blood lines of both Mary and Joseph were similar up through King David, and then the family lines divided. By implication, Mary and Joseph can both claim these grandmothers from many generations in the past.

Matthew's good news reminds us that Jesus, on his human side, is a mixed racial person. He shed his blood *for* the world on Good Friday, but he got that blood *from* the world. The grandmothers belong in the Christmas crèche and in our mission message. The opening paragraph of the New Testament is good news. It rules out any claim to racial or ethnic superiority. Eduard Schweizer of Zurich observed in his Matthew commentary that these birth stories have mission significance.[10] They remind us that not only does the fruit of God's good news go beyond the boundaries of Israel and the Jewish people, but so also do the roots of the Gospel. The message of Jesus was designed all along to be inclusive, showing God's intentional love for *all* peoples.

There is more to this story. Matthew includes the record of that terrible massacre of all the baby boys of Bethlehem,

---

[10] Eduard Schweizer, *The Good News According to Matthew*, tran. David E. Green (Atlanta: John Knox Press, 1975).

and of Rachel, Mother of Israel, weeping for another generation of lost boys. She wept first when she stood by the road and watched Nebuchadnezzar march all the royal sons off to Babylon in three successive sieges of Jerusalem: 606, 597 and finally 586 BC. How could there ever be a king again in Jerusalem with all those kids taken and never heard from again? She wept again when King Herod commanded the killing of all baby boys, two years old and under, in Bethlehem.

But that is not the end of Matthew's Christmas story. First, he wants us to know that one of those Jewish kids, Daniel, mastered the Chaldean culture and language while rejecting the life style and values of the king and palace. Sometime in his life I believe he edited a clay tablet for future astronomers, pointing out that someday a star would appear in the sky over Bethlehem, where a very special king would be born. Six hundred years later, Babylonian scholars came searching. Matthew wants us to know those kids were not just victims. They were on mission. They told truth to power, and nearly six centuries later, not the army, but worshipers arrived in Jerusalem.

Finally, Matthew wants Rachel, as well as all others, to know that the special baby born King of the Jews escaped Herod, returned after several years in Egypt, lived in Nazareth and Galilee, and went to Jerusalem, where on his cross Roman soldiers could nail a title above his head in three languages: Hebrew, Greek, and Latin. "Jesus Christ, King of the Jews." Weep no more, Rachel. One grave is empty. The King is coming!

For me, the story gets more personal. Our adopted African American son once told me that his birth mother never told him who his father was. She had four children, two girls in Mississippi and two boys in Chicago, but she never named his father. Brian told us about going up and down

58

Chicago streets searching for men who looked like him. The way he put it had a punch line. "Which pimp is my dad?" Later, he told me that I was his only father. That bond is very special. When Brian joined our family in 1977, I began to study and preach on texts that might provide hope for him. There are several, but Matthew is special.

PART II: THE MISSION TRAIL

BARNABAS OF CYPRUS

Died c. 61

BARNABAS OF CYPRUS

Barnabas of Cyprus was a recognized and trusted leader in the early church. He is mentioned twenty-two times by Luke in the book of Acts. Barnabas seems to have sold land in Cyprus in order to provide funding for food in Jerusalem after Pentecost. He was well positioned with relatives living in Jerusalem. The family of his cousin Mark may have provided the house with the upper room used for Jesus' Passover meal with his disciples before his trial and death.

When reports arrived in Jerusalem that the church in Antioch was successfully reaching and receiving Gentiles into their midst, Barnabas was sent north to investigate. When he got there, he rejoiced at this new stage of church witness.[11] He designed the international pastoral leadership team mentioned in Acts: two Africans, two Asians, and a European-trained Jew named Saul of Tarsus.[12]

Perhaps only Barnabas could have built a bridge of trust to Saul, who had terrorized the church in Jerusalem and elsewhere. But Saul had experienced a remarkable conversion, plus a complete theological re-orientation. Barnabas sought out Saul, and for a year helped mentor him in Antioch, before that church commissioned both of them to undertake a missionary journey. At Barnabas' suggestion, they also took Mark, who apparently lost interest and did not complete the mission.

---

[11] Acts 11: 20-23
[12] Acts 13:1

At their return to Jerusalem for the first church council,[13] Barnabas demonstrated leadership. There may still have been a reluctance to accept Paul's leadership by a group of Christians who had suffered at his hand in the past. When Barnabas suggested they take Mark on the second mission trip, Paul vehemently opposed the idea, causing them to split up and choose separate travel companions. Paul took Silas and started out on his second missionary journey; Barnabas took Mark and went to Cyprus. Scripture never mentions Barnabas again, but the Greek Orthodox Church of Cyprus identified Barnabas as the first bishop of their church.

A great missionary evangelist, E. Stanley Jones, has suggested that while Paul was a *truth apostle*, Barnabas was a *grace apostle*. Obviously Paul needed grace as much or more than anyone alive in those days, but he became so focused on truth and integrity in mission that he had no patience with Mark. Barnabas was more than willing to take his younger cousin along and mentor him in ministry.

Barnabas means "Son of Consolation." Everything we know of his forgiving and reconciling life confirms the fact that he fulfilled the meaning of his name.

At times in Christian history, grace and truth ceased being two sides of the coin and become rival denominations. This happened in North Africa in the third and fourth centuries, when churches preached against each other, rather than reaching out to the needy or the lost in their societies. We see evidence of that in our own cities today.

Paul, pursuing truth in his early letter written to the Galatians, suggested that Barnabas was too close to his Jewish roots to accept the cultural freedom of non-Jewish

---

[13] Acts 15

Christians.[14] A few years later, Paul commended
Barnabas' example of working to support himself in
mission, as Paul did in Corinth.[15] Later, Paul and Mark
were reconciled in Rome, a fact based on Paul's comment
to the Colossians: "If [Mark] comes to you, welcome
him."[16] In Philemon, Paul salutes Mark as a "fellow
minister."[17] Papias, an early church historian, said: "Mark
wrote Peter's preaching as he preached it."[18] Evidence in
Scripture and early writings verifies that Mark was
reconciled to both great leaders, Peter and Paul, before
their deaths around 64 AD.

For me, the crowning tribute to Barnabas is that Mark did
not fail on his second mission journey, when he went to
Alexandria to strengthen that great church. Meanwhile,
according to Eusebius of Caesarea (260-340), father of
church history, Barnabas served as bishop in Cyprus until
his death.

Today, Mark is buried in the crypt under the altar of St.
Mark's Coptic Orthodox Church in Cairo, a tomb I often
visit with my students. As we marvel that the bones of
Mark are there in our midst, I give special commendation
and thanks for Barnabas and his servant leadership which
involved mentoring both Paul and Mark for their
respective missions.

The Lord knows that many of us need reconciling leaders.
I have known many in my life and ministry. They have a

---

[14] Galations 2:13

[15] 1 Corinthians 9:6

[16] Colossians 4:10

[17] Philemon verse 24

[18] See Paphias (c. AD 140), quoted in Eusebius
HE.iii.39.15; Irenaeus, *Adv. Haer*.iii 1.2.

capacity to overlook personal faults for the sake of large Kingdom issues. Barnabas was such a person.

POLYCARP OF SMYRNA

70 to 155 or 156

olycarp may have been the leading Christian of the second century in Roman Asia, known today as Turkey. He was a great defender of Orthodox Christianity and serves as a link between the Apostles of the first century and the Apostolic Fathers who emerged late in the second and third centuries. He seems to have known the Elder John, the "beloved disciple" of Jesus, and long time church leader in Ephesus. He traveled more than once to Rome to meet key leaders, and also to refute those persons he thought were not true to the biblical faith.

We have few details from the many years of his life and service, but historians acknowledge the early influence of Ignatius on Polycarp, whose witness eventually meant martyrdom. The Greek word for witness is the word *martyr*. It is not difficult to see how the first known Christian martyr, Stephen, may have influenced the tradition. There is only one reference in the New Testament to Jesus standing in heaven, and many of us believe he stood to receive Stephen.[19]

Under Roman Emperors like Trajan and Pliny, the persecution of those who refused to worship the emperors accelerated. Christians were touted as atheists for their belief in an unseen God. When the authorities first came for Polycarp, he fled for a brief time, but he was found and realized that God had chosen him for martyrdom.

The proconsul who presided over the trial, tried to dissuade Polycarp, reminding him of his old age, and promising that if he would just worship the emperor, he

---

[19] Acts 7:56

would be set free. Polycarp was not persuaded.
Apparently with loud voice he proclaimed: "For eighty-six
years I have served him, and he has done me no evil. How
can I curse my King who saved me?"

When threatened with fire by the judge, he replied that the
fire the judge could light would last but a moment,
whereas the eternal fire would never go out. Tied to a post
as the fire was lit, he was reported to have said, "Lord
Sovereign God . . . I thank you that you have deemed me
worthy of this moment, so that, jointly with your martyrs, I
may have a share in the cup of Christ." *The Martyrdom of
Polycarp* was a well-attested document and circulated
around the Roman Empire, influencing countless
thousands over many centuries. Such documents made
their way into the *Ecclesiastical History iv.15* of Eusebius,
a major source of early Christian history.

Martyrdom became a major topic in biographical writings
through the centuries. From Justin Martyr's *Life,* dating
from the second century (d.160), *Foxes Book of Martyrs*
that appeared in sixteenth century England (1563), and
from many present day stories, we know that *the blood of
martyrs is the seed of the church*, a major factor in the
spread of mission. According to some contemporary
mission scholars, there may be far more Christian martyrs
in the twentieth century than in the first nineteen centuries
combined, a fact that is less-well known.

While in high school, I was personally influenced by five
young Wheaton graduates who were martyred at the hands
of Auca tribesmen in Ecuador. What happened afterwards
was even more significant for my life. Betty Elliott, one of
the widows, went to live for two years among the Aucas,
taking along her beautiful little three-year old blond
daughter. You can read that story in *The Savage My
Kinsman.* My two-year old blond son Brian could have

been taken for Valerie Elliott's twin when we moved into inner city Chicago in 1965.

That is when I learned of a dichotomy among many American Christians. When you take your children into dangerous foreign mission fields, you are called a hero, very spiritual, a great example of devotion. But when you raise your children in violent inner city neighborhoods, you can be called a masochist hurting your kids. The foreign missionaries were a great example to me. While they may have had cobras and pythons in their yards, I had Cobras, Pythons, Latin Kings, TJO, and other gangs in my neighborhood. I believe, if God has called you, that the safest place to raise your children is in the very place where you have been called. For us it was inner city Chicago for thirty-five years.

GREGORY OF ARMENIA

240 to 332

We know there were Christians in Armenia before Gregory, called *The Illuminator*, arrived late in the third century from Cappadocia in modern Turkey. Tertullian attributes some of the first century witness to a missionary known as Addai.[20] Nevertheless, Gregory the Illuminator is remembered as the Apostle to Armenia. Armenia is celebrated, almost universally, as the first Christian nation, dating from 301.

Gregory seems to have come from royalty, son of a Parthian who murdered King Khosrov I of Armenia. Forced to flee into exile, his family went to Cappadocia where later Gregory became a Christian. He returned to Armenia about 280. After more than a decade of imprisonment for his faith and witness, he emerged to lead Armenian King Tiridates III to Christianity. The Bishop of Caesarea consecrated Gregory as Bishop in Syria. When he returned to Armenia, he wore the Armenian title: *Catholicos.*

In 301 AD, Christianity was made the official religion of the empire. Armenians are proud of their designation as the "first Christian nation," but Syrians have long disputed that claim with a counter claim that Odessa, now part of modern Syria, was the first Christian nation, a fact

---

[20] For an introduction to Tertullian, see *The Library of Christian Classics,* Vol. V: *Early Latin Theology: Selections from Tertullian, Cyprian, Ambrose, and Jerome,* trans. and ed. S. L. Greenslade (Philadelphia: Westminster Press, 1956).

supported by Kenneth Scott Latourette.[21] Last year, in the Middle East, I heard a brilliant historical lecture by the Armenian Archbishop of Iraq. He holds the traditional view that Armenia was the first nation to adopt Christianity. As a result, I have not seen enough evidence to warrant changing my traditional view. I was pleased to have my own personal celebration of the seventeen hundredth anniversary of 301 on this mission trail at Bakken in 2001.

Armenia must surely have suffered more persecutions per capita than any other people, as army after army marched through their ancient mountain lands. Despite official denial by Turkey, historians all know about the Holocaust perpetrated on Armenia by Turks in 1915, when western nations were preoccupied with WWI. More than one million were killed, whole cities were destroyed, and Armenians were scattered all over the world.

I visited the Armenian Church and cemetery in Dacca, Bangladesh, and learned that Armenians labored as missionaries along the Silk Road into ancient India. Early translations of the Bible into Armenian date from the fourth century. Armenian church leaders participated in the earliest church councils.

In 450 AD, when Persians tried to impose their own religion on this Christian country, Armenians hoped the Romans would come to their aid, and put 1036 men into the mountain passes to defend the country. But the Romans never arrived. One year later, not surprisingly, the Armenians rejected the Council of Chalcedon definition of the two natures of Christ. Like Copts in

---

[21] Kenneth Scott Latourette, *A History of The Expansion of Christianity: The First Five Centuries*, Vol. I (Grand Rapids MI: Zondervan, 1970), pp. 105 ff.

Egypt and Ethiopia, Syrians and Assyrians, these groups are called Oriental Orthodox and nicknamed *Monophysites*, or people who believe Jesus had one divine-human nature, rather than two natures.

The Armenian experience of national or cultural conversion, mandated by a king or emperor, became a pattern in western Europe after the baptism of Clovis, King of the Franks in 496 AD.[22] Generally, these historic churches – Catholic and Orthodox – seek to work toward the center and upward to the powerful. Protestant missionaries have a different starting point. They usually begin with individual conversions, often at the edges of the culture with the poor or marginalized.

Nearly two thousand years after Christ, many modern Protestant and Evangelical missionaries are realizing the benefits of starting the evangelization process by working with the whole of the tribe and the acknowledged leaders. When individual converts are stripped away from their cultures, they often set up churches in alien subcultures where growth is impossible.

Do we start at the edge of a group and work in, or do we start at the center of power and work out? In truth, the church has done both over many centuries, and a case can be made for either.

My Norwegian church heritage models the group approach. Government approved and sponsored Lutheran churches ruled religious life in Norway after the Reformation. But I am also a product of the Prayer House

---

[22] Roland H. Bainton, *Christendom: A Short History of Christianity and Its Impact on Western Civilization,* Vol. I: *From the Birth of Christ to the Reformation* (NY: Harper & Row, 1966), p. 145 ff.

Movement influenced by Inner Mission societies that appeared in Germany and later came to Scandinavia. Those lay leaders added personal sanctification, personal faith, and mission to official Lutheran beliefs. A tension has always existed between these two approaches to being Christian within the same cultural framework.

I have come to value both the Armenian Orthodox and the Armenian Evangelical traditions, and the hosts of scholars and missionaries those churches have produced to enrich us all. McCormick Seminary in Chicago, where I did two degrees and taught history as an adjunct professor for several years, had a strong Armenian legacy with historian Joseph Haroutunian, from whom I benefited much on my own journey.

I remember a lunch with two well-known Chicago City Council members: my own alderman, Richard Mell; and Alderman Hagopian from a nearby ward. When I had a chance to tell the Armenian alderman how much I admired his church and his history, his eyes filled with tears and his voice broke. He said: "You know about my church? Many people in Chicago think Armenian is a disease."

A decade before Constantine conquered Rome in 312, and declared Christianity officially legal in the Roman Empire in 313, Gregory the Illuminator baptized the King of Armenia, changing the world and Christian history. I thank God for the lingering witness and mission of the Armenian Church.

FRUMENTIUS OF ETHIOPIA

300 to 380

FRUMENTIUS OF ETHIOPIA

The Bible refers to Ethiopia forty-two times. I noted that with surprise in 1990 while preparing for my first of several visits to that country. Ever since my early New Testament studies, a lingering question regarding the eighth chapter of Acts remained unsolved, where an Ethiopian is found reading an Isaiah scroll written in classical Hebrew dating from the eighth century BC. How, I asked, did this man, who lived two thousand miles from Israel near modern day Eritrea on the north coast of Africa, know classical Hebrew? An Ethiopian professor gave me the answer. "That's easy," said the professor, "he was Jewish. He was a descendent of King Solomon and the Queen of Sheba from the tenth century BC."

A Falasha Jewish community of black Jews has existed in Ethiopia for centuries and traces its history with two taproots. The first, the Hebraic tradition, begins with Solomon in the ninth century BC and includes the first century story of the eunuch who could read Hebrew. The second tap root dates from the fourth century AD and is the reason for the 4th stake on the mission trail.

In 323 AD two young Syrian brothers –Frumentius and Edessius – were captured and put aboard a ship returning from India. Spared the death inflicted on all the other captives, they were taken to the palace in Axum, the ancient capitol of Ethiopia. There they lived, perhaps assigned as babysitters or tutors to the young and future king, Edzana, whom they led to faith in Jesus.

Archaeologists have found coins from Edzana's empire with crosses on them. I have seen those coins and other artifacts in the Ethiopian Church Museum. Just two years ago, the current eighty-year-old Patriarch, Abuna Paulus, gave my seminar in Addis Ababa a guided tour of this recently expanded museum.

After more than two amazing decades of mission and ministry in this region, Frumentius decided he would return to Syria. He stopped along the way in Alexandria, Egypt, to report to the Coptic Orthodox Patriarch, Athenasius, and ask that a bishop be appointed and sent back. Athenasius immediately appointed Frumentius and sent him back to fill that position. That explains the rather paternalistic relationship the Egyptians had to the Ethiopians until the modern era, when finally the Ethiopians became completely self-governing, or *autocephalic*, as they say in Orthodox circles.

For two hundred years, or until Islam arose in Arabia just across the gulf, Ethiopia was an amazing and thriving missionary church. In time, Islam closed the straights and roads to Christian traffic, and the capital was moved further into this mountain kingdom. However, Ethiopia, roughly twice the size of France, remained predominately Christian, surrounded by a sea of Islam on all sides. Many monks came to this Abyssinian Kingdom in the fifth and sixth centuries, exiled (scholars say) because they, like the Egyptians and Armenians, could not agree to the Council of Chalcedon's words on the two natures of Christ in 451 AD.

About the time of Luther, Moslems tried for thirty years to conquer and rule Ethiopia and were eventually expelled by the Portuguese. But they in turn were also expelled after sending in the Jesuits with a mandate to bring Roman Catholic theology to the country.

Jember Teferra, a niece of Haile Selessie, the last Ethiopian emperor, has become my window on this country for the past twenty years, since our meeting in 1989. She married another Haile, also from royalty, who, after receiving his Ph.D. in engineering from Carnegie Mellon University in Pittsburgh, became the mayor of Addis Ababa with the mandate to make it a capitol worthy of all African nations. In the coup that killed the Patriarch and the Emperor, Jember's husband went to prison for eight years. She carried meals to him twice daily, all the while continuing her work at the local hospital. Then she was arrested and imprisoned without charge for five years. Friends took their four children to safety in England. The government confiscated their house and made it the Cuban embassy. Only recently was it returned.

When they were finally released from prison, Jember and Haile joined their children in Manchester, where she did a master's degree in community and economic development, focused on the abject poverty of more than forty thousand slum dwellers. Her husband died before she could finish her doctoral degree with me. She faces continual harassment by many officials, but she persists.

We have taught together over the years. She grew up Orthodox and was married in the Emperor's church with his blessing. She has become a Kingdom-focused Evangelical of Orthodox background who never left that church, but has worked for its renewal in many ways over a long time. The Patriarch jokes with her about when they were both in prison at the same time. He ate cookies in her kitchen when he was young.

Here is a brief status report from my seminar there in 2007. There are thirty-five million Orthodox Christians in the Ethiopian church, about half the national population. There are 500,000 priests in this church, equal to the population of Seattle. There are fifteen hundred monasteries, eleven training schools, two theological seminaries, and *no money* to sustain all this. Since 1974, hostile governments have taken their lands. With wars in Eritrea in the north and most recently in Somalia on the east, the country has seen a dramatic growth of Islam, aggressively funded by Saudi Arabia. The Orthodox blame Evangelical missionaries for their "sheep stealing" approaches, yet there is evidence that renewal and dialogue has increased. Catholic, Lutheran, Mennonite and other recent denominations are working more closely together.

Jember has been to Bakken several times in recent years. I have told her this 4th stake is also for her.

PATRICK OF IRELAND

389 to 461

Patrick was born into a family on the west coast of Britain. We learn from his own writings that while his grandfather and father were Christians and held church titles, his own faith lay dormant. At age sixteen, in 405, he was captured by a Scottish raiding party and taken as a slave to Ireland. For six years he herded animals, and through that experience returned to his Christian faith. Responding to a vision, he escaped to the coast and boarded a ship that landed in southern France. After months of wandering, he entered a monastery where he studied for three years.

Patrick went back to Britain and joyously reunited with his family, but his call to mission – to follow Jesus' command to go – had become the priority of his life. When he returned to Ireland in 432 and was appointed a bishop, he did not stay in a diocese or live as a leader among Christians. His new calling was to the totally pagan territories of the north, and later to the wildwest and southeast. He planted monasteries, most often led by the local elites whom he had won to faith in Christ, and encouraged scholarship and arts in all of them. Rather than attempting to do his own studies in Gaelic, he brought Latin to Ireland. He explained his own imperfect Latin as the result of waiting too long to become a scholar.

When Patrick died in 461, Irish Christianity had adapted to a rural land of no cities and towns through contextualized monasticism that attracted youths in unprecedented numbers. In time a vibrant Celtic mission explosion led to Iona, to missions beyond into Britain and the Continent, and, some say, to places across the ocean.

The Roman Empire gradually disintegrated during Patrick's life. Ireland had never been a part of it. Amazingly, Ireland became a model of extending the Christian faith without martyrs, bishops, and great churches, and certainly without armies and violence. The Irish monasteries did not function as islands of cultural escape for the spiritual elites, but were as small hamlets within a land of villages, where whole communities of men went to sea to fish. It turns out that monasteries were much more portable than solid stone churches with fixed parish structures.

Patrick reported in his *Confessions* and other writings that he faced the opposition of Druids, the major religion of Britain and Ireland. Early on he realized that if he could reach local pagan leaders with the faith, they could become his disciples, be trained as abbots, and bring a Christian values-shaped rule to this rural nation where populations migrated to work on farms or on the seas. He baptized thousands and even consecrated church leadership. Today we call this contextualization.

Some of us might question the imposition of Latin and continental scholarship on rural Ireland. One ironic result is that as the people became bilingual in Latin, they continued to speak native Gaelic and retained the purity of both languages. In contrast, church-imposed Latin on the Continent gradually morphed into Italian, French, Spanish, and other Romance languages. It was the Irish missionaries who reintroduced a more pure church-Latin back into Europe in later centuries.

The Irish mission vitality that emerged from Patrick had a more balanced view of creation and redemption than the pure Augustinian salvation emphasis. This has made it very appealing to youth in Europe today. Patrick would be called a Charismatic for his belief that the Holy Spirit is actively at work in cultures before missionaries arrive. The Celtic symbol of the Holy Spirit became a wild goose in flight, uncontrolled and unpredictable.

Patrick also reminds us that while cross-boundary and cross-cultural missionary work takes place beyond the pale of traditional churches and cultural norms, benefits may show up later, even centuries later. Irish spirituality led to a different hairstyle. All clergy were supposed to look angelic in traditional hairstyles: some by shaving bald; others with a fringe around the bald top. The Irish-cut was as though you had put a bowl on the head and cut around it. More significantly, they had a different date for Easter. All those things got settled in 664 at the Synod of Whitby in England, where the Irish lost to the Romans. But when paganism again became active on the Continent, Irish Celtic missionaries came to renew the faith of Europe.[23]

I see this happening today. Missionaries left Europe and North America for Latin America, Asia, and Africa to plant the church at a time when up to eighty percent of the world's Christians were white, northern and western. Today, by far the majority of Christians are non-white, non-northern, and non-western, and they are sending radical missionaries back to re-evangelize the secularized west. The legacy of missions could not have been imagined when the pioneers left responsibilities at home to go abroad on mission. Who would have imagined that by leaving they would end up saving the people at home? It is a Kingdom phenomena.

---

[23] Dale T. Irvin & Scott W. Sunquist: *History of the World Christian Movement,* Vol. I: *Earliest Christianity to 1453* (Maryknoll NY: Orbis Books, 2004), pp. 236-237.

BENEDICT OF NURSIA

480 to 550

F ew would dispute the claim that what Augustine was to theology in the Roman church, Benedict was to spirituality in the monasteries. Ironically, he does not appear to have been ordained, and there is little evidence that he ever intended to establish an order. He was so turned off by the deteriorating Christianity he found during his study years in Rome, that he withdrew to live as a hermit in a cave. Others joined him and out of this following twelve small monastic communities were formed, each with an abbot appointed by Benedict. Eventually they asked him to leave. He migrated with a few men to found Monte Cassino, about half way between Rome and Naples, where he remained until his death, and where he is buried alongside his sister, St. Scolastica.

From this hill, where he could look down on the valley below, he collected ideas from previous monastic leaders, and made a handbook called *The Rule*, to guide his followers. Everyone would live in a disciplined community, not as hermits or vagabonds. To the vows of poverty, chastity, and obedience, he added silence and stability. Every monastery would be self-funded and therefore every monk would work. Over time this resulted in growth of income and sustainable living around all the monasteries.

The overarching goal for each monastery was not comfort, but worship and praise of God. Monks rose at two in the morning for three hours of worship and meditation. At five they began four hours of mandatory study. At nine they went to work in the fields. At noon, they returned to eat one of two cooked meals for the day. After an hour of rest they returned to the fields. After *compline*, the final prayers of the day, they went to bed at six. Each monk received a few items to mend his clothing, but otherwise, everything was held in common. Benedict's *Rule* was designed to govern communities focused on spirituality and was not intended to affect mission, scholarship, economic development, or creation of wealth. Eventually the Benedictine monasteries impacted each of those realities.

In a disintegrating civilization, mountain top monasteries appeared irrelevant to invaders, who initially treated them with contempt. Gradually, the lonely newcomers found that humble monks had the gift of hospitality. Over time monasteries became welcoming and teaching centers for the secular population. Self-ruled as well as self-funded, brothers elected an abbot and then observed strict obedience. The organized church, at first, had no idea that those fixed monastic centers, with a rule that monks were not to travel, could ever be a mission agency. But when churches lost the capacity to send their own trained and funded missionaries, the spread of monasteries became the heart of mission strategy for Europe, as it had in Egypt and elsewhere. Once churches could survive in cities and even thrive – becoming wealthy and worldly – deserts, caves, and mountaintops beckoned many of the faithful. Lay movements multiplied and soon produced monasteries for devoted women as well, living in communities under discipline.

Eastern monasticism placed a higher value on solitude, often rivaling the institutional church. Western monasticism was more practical and always maintained contact with surrounding communities. The monasteries were not threatening to the official church until later, when their independence and wealth promoted powerful abbots, but that was centuries after Benedict.

When Gregory the Great became the first great mediaeval Pope (in 590), he established foreign missions and had his missionaries take copies of the *Rule* with them. By 800, Charlemagne also demonstrated respect for the monks by promoting education. While cathedral schools in city parishes became significant to scholarship, the monks who copied manuscripts, translated classics, and valued learning were equally significant in preserving and expanding cultural and learning centers.

Historian Kenneth Scott Latourette observed a parallel monastic movement happening within Buddhism.[24] While monastic Christianity spread around Europe, engaging new frontiers in the north and west, Buddhism escaped India and spread in monastic fashion into China, Japan, and elsewhere in Asia. He sees no links between them, but speculates that what may have been happening contextually in each location, possibly created the seeds for growth of new religions in new territories. Christianity and Buddhism both spread without military assistance, at a time when existing institutions were fragmenting.

Monasticism, however organized, creates a tension for the church. Is the church a transformer of culture, or an alternative to the culture? The very success of the monasteries, creating wealth and power, got them into trouble later, requiring reforms and new kinds of monastic structures. Monks, however organized, at times critiqued the official church, and at times partnered with it (as in the Crusades), reminding us that in this world of sin and struggle, it is hard to get our structures right all the time.

---

[24] *A History of The Expansion of Christianity,* Vol. II, *The Thousand Years of Uncertainty: A.D. 500 – 1500 A.D.* (Grand Rapids MI: Zondervan, 1970), pp. 277 ff.

ALOPEN OF CHINA

Who arrived in Xian in 635

History is not an exact science. Instead, it is a point of view: a view from a point, usually the vantage point of the writer. Benedict is still the key mission person of the seventh century, given his role in western Catholic and monastic history. But I seriously considered Alopen, the Nestorian missionary from Syria.

While Benedict was drafting his *Rule,* and Mohammad was winding down (he died in 632), the Nestorian mission – traveling the Silk Road from Baghdad to China – arrived in 635. They had been twenty years on their journey.

Alopen, who seems to have learned Chinese and showed up with images including a cross plus the Scriptures, soon found favor with the Tang Dynasty Emperor T'ai-tsung. Alopen was granted permission to translate parts of the Bible – including the Ten Commandments – into Chinese, and had Chinese scholars assigned to him in the Emperor's library of over 200,000 manuscripts. He also was given permission to form monasteries, apparently a dozen of them in cities of western China. Because Buddhism had become the established religion of the empire at that time, Alopen developed a dialogue style and presented his Christian faith with contextual creativity.

Zoroastrianism from Persia had also come to China, along with other religions. Toleration to all foreign religions ended after 845. Only in the past ten years are we discovering that the influence of the Nestorian missionaries was far greater than originally supposed. A stone stele with Christian inscriptions was found outside

Xian and still resides there in a museum with hundreds of other ancient steles.

Our BGU annual China seminar includes a trip to Xian. For the past five years we have traveled the half-day journey out into the countryside past the museum that houses the terracotta soldiers discovered in 1976. We have made our way by foot up a steep hill to a non-descript town and farm, to what seemed like a Buddhist pagoda. Next we climbed up a shaky makeshift ladder and entered this leaning pagoda at about the third level. On the walls we found frescos of Bible stories, including Jonah, the Nestorian's favorite missionary. It is easy to understand the power of the Jonah story, teaching that God's love and forgiveness went far beyond the borders of ancient Israel.

We now know that this pagoda was originally seven stories high. The Christian stele was found on this site in the seventeenth century, but the pagoda remained unexplored until this decade. These discoveries from antiquity prove that Christians were in western China for five hundred years before Marco Polo, and before the Catholic mission arrived in the 1200's.

Today, China has the second largest Christian population of any country in the world. At the rate evangelization is happening, China will become the world's largest Christian population about the time when it overtakes the USA in economic power, perhaps before 2040. Christians in China already outnumber communist party members.

I predict that the Christian history of China will be re-written to show that it was not by gunboats from the west that missionaries first came, but by overland routes traveled by Armenian traders and Baghdad monks like Alopen. The Asian-born baby Jesus is very much at home in Asia today, but has been for many centuries. We must all learn to write Christian history from a global rather than a traditional western perspective. Christianity is not a white or western religion, but bias dies hard.

JOHN OF DAMASCUS

660 to 749

JOHN OF DAMASCUS

After Mohammad's death in 632, the leadership of Islam split into two traditions with a civil war that ended with the death of Ali and his Shiite partisans. Muawiya moved his hereditary caliphate out of Persia to Damascus and the Umayyad era of Islam ruled until 750. John's life and career parallel Islam's arrival in Damascus as a new power.

Byzantine Christianity, puffed up with importance following the 451 Council of Chalcedon victory over Oriental Orthodox Christians, mistreated Egyptian, Syrian and Persian Christians, burdening them with oppressive tax, land, and war policies. Islam freed them from that oppression, making them quite happy with the early occupation and eventual rule by Muslims.

I remember my shock in 1976 in Cairo when I heard a Christian historian say that the Christians of Egypt encouraged the Arabs to conquer them as a way to throw out the oppressive Byzantine Christians. In 1984 in Dacca, Bangladesh, a Muslim scholar told me that the reason Pakistan and Bangladesh split from Hindu India was because the Delhi Brahman Hindus treated the low caste Hindus in those "river culture countries" like dirt. When Muslim traders came and treated them like brothers, all converted to Islam, and within a hundred years the map of Asia changed.

John's father had the highly significant job of representing all Christians to the Caliph. John stepped into that role as well. Besides studying Greek from age twelve, he enrolled in Arabic school where he studied the Koran and was encouraged to memorize it. In 716, he withdrew from public life compelled by his faith (or pressure from outsiders, perhaps the Byzantine Patriarch) and entered Mar Saba Monastery near Jerusalem to study as a monk. He wrote comprehensively in all areas of theology and is sometimes called the last of the great fathers or doctors of the Eastern Orthodox churches.

John was also the first theologian to engage Islam honestly and explain it to Christians. Having done that, surprisingly, he wrote a very strong critique of Islam that he called the *Ishmaelite Heresy*. Some say it is a polemic on Islam.

Seeing the impossibility of separating God, Word, and Spirit to Muslims, he avoided calling Jesus *Son of God*. To Muslims who see the Cross as an idol, he suggested it was no more so than the Kaaba, so highly revered by them. He was critical of polygamy as practiced in Islam. His Christian scholarship was more encyclopedic than original. He borrowed heavily from his favorite Cappadocian, Gregory of Nazianzus. However, John's book – *Fount of Knowledge* – became a work of lasting importance in the east and also in the west after its discovery by twelfth century western scholars.[25]

Eastern Christians are Easter people. All through history, faith and hope emerges in their resurrection hymns. Here are four verses of the famous Easter hymn written by John of Damascus.[26]

---

[25] For an introduction and basic bibliography, see articles on John of Damascus in *The Oxford Dictionary of the Christian Church*, ed. F. L. Cross (London: Oxford Press, 1966), and *The New International Dictionary of the Christian Church*, Rev. Ed., J. D. Douglas, Gen. Ed. (Grand Rapids: Zondervan, 1979)
[26] Tran. John Mason Neale (d. 1866).

Come, ye faithful, raise the strain
   of triumphant gladness!
God hath brought his Israel
   into joy from sadness:
loosed from Pharaoh's bitter yoke
   Jacob's sons and daughters,
led them with un-moistened foot
   through the Red Sea waters.

'Tis the spring of souls today:
   Christ hath burst his prison,
and from three days' sleep in death
   as a sun hath risen;
all the winter of our sins,
   long and dark, is flying
from his light, to whom we give
   laud and praise undying.

Now the queen of seasons, bright
   with the day of splendor,
with the royal feast of feasts,
   comes its joy to render;
comes to glad Jerusalem,
   who with true affection
welcomes in unwearied strains,
   Jesus' resurrection.

Neither might the gates of death,
   nor the tomb's dark portal,
nor the watchers, nor the seal
   hold thee as a mortal:
but today amidst thine own
   thou didst stand, bestowing
that thy peace which evermore
   passeth human knowing.

Now, with mosques appearing alongside churches in all our cities, it is time for seminaries to recover the tradition of John of Damascus. We must teach students the significance of Jesus mentioned more than ninety times in the Koran, so that we have a common starting point for a Christian-Muslim dialogue about Jesus.

BONIFACE OF GERMANY

680 to 754

No less a scholar than Stephen Neill called Boniface the greatest of all missionaries during the so called Dark Ages of Europe. He was born and grew up in England, but his mission call took him to Frisia (Netherlands today), where he faced strong opposition and few results. In Rome, Pope Gregory consecrated him bishop for the German frontier, but before going, he secured pledges of financial support from key Roman bishops. That made possible church expansion far beyond the current borders of Roman Europe, and inaugurated a new foreign mission strategy.

Like Elijah of old, he began by settling whose god was to be feared and worshiped. The Germans had a sacred tree, a symbol of their gods. All understood that if it were cut down, that person would be destroyed. Boniface took an ax to it. When he was not destroyed, the populations north of the Rhine understood that his God was indeed the true God. Christianity spread among the Germanic peoples. Subsequently, he installed bishops in Fulda and many other cities. He was so gifted in organizing churches that he was asked to help out in the Frankish Kingdom as well. He became a kingmaker when he crowned Pepin.

Prior to Boniface, European churches baptized mostly at Easter and Pentecost. He is credited with setting up a discipleship system that had as its goal turning those persons who were Christians in name, only into persons who truly practiced their faith every day. In terms of faith and culture, he did not try to destroy all pre-Christian cultural and religious beliefs, but sought to transform them. The German church started adding events, seasons, and festivals, which had the effect of creating a liturgical year. Rather than force Latin on everyday common speech, Boniface affirmed the local languages. That led to the diversity of languages and cultures present in today's church. He preserved unity through Latin scholarship and Roman architecture.

Predictably, tensions surfaced between diocesan bishops in French territories and those in German territories. Boniface, the roving missionary authority, with papal approval, crossed many local and regional boundaries. When Boniface was made Bishop of Mainz, at age seventy or so, some thought the jurisdictional issues were solved. But ever the missionary, Boniface decided to go one more time to Frisia to extend his evangelistic work. His party was attacked and as all were being killed, he cheerfully encouraged his colleagues to praise God. They would soon be with Christ and the saints forever.

Missiology is what we call the study of and the strategy for the world mission of the church. This discipline has grown primarily in the past two hundred years as Christianity went global, often led by westerners, and often with the assistance of western governments, colonization, funding or military cover. What happens to mission structures once churches are planted and take responsibility for self-propagating, self-governing, and self-supporting? A robust conversation of Protestant and Catholic scholars has been going strong and we have had a host of instructive conferences, schools, associations, and international covenants around the issues. Today we might define mission as "to, in, and from all six continents." Comity agreements were put in place nearly one hundred years ago between mission societies and denominations, whereby missions agreed to work in specific regions and not all pile into the same areas. That agreement hoped to avoid competition between mission agencies and established churches.

104

In my ministry lifetime, the phrase *unreached peoples* came into focus and definition, largely through the indefatigable work of the late Ralph Winter. He, with many others, lamented the institutionalization of missions into fixed structures that locked missionaries into maintenance. Many mission organizations now have plans to sell or give away their hospitals, schools, and headquarters, and to focus totally on the unreached that used to be in jungles but now are mostly in cities.

Some emerging Christian and mission leaders in the southern regions of Latin America, Asia, and Africa, find that the old missionaries did not leave. They just withdrew from local church, mission, or denominational accountability structures, and they operate side by side in cities without any regard for the churches that are already there. Some local people cry, "Foul!"

But that is only part of the story. The fastest growing mission enterprises today are from the regions of the global south. They come with a vibrant faith that resembles the faith they received from western missionaries one hundred years ago, a faith long diminished in the secular west; and they are planting churches in the former sending mission countries of America and Europe faster than anyone expected. I join scholars such as Andrew Walls and Phillip Jenkins who celebrate the emerging mission paradigms: new patterns of mission coming from south to north rather than west to east; the shift from an Atlantic to a Pacific perimeter world; and countries like China and Nigeria becoming centers of mission by sending rather than receiving. Back in 1908, German scholar Martin Kahler coined the aphorism: "mission is the mother of theology." Every theological category will be impacted when people in non-western cultures read the Bible with fresh insight. Boniface introduced these tensions into Europe more than a thousand years ago. We will struggle with them more than ever in years to come.[27]

Structures of mission are a huge topic in mission studies. Many traditional structures have been unjust or patronizing. Other mission structures reveal values that come from old Marine images: *Take the hill! Dam the torpedos! Full speed ahead! Eternity is coming! Souls hang in the balance!* Obviously we must carefully sort out issues of motives from issues of methods in each case.

In my work with the International Lausanne Committee, where I was Senior Associate for Large Cities from 1979 to 1999, I saw a very natural tension between evangelists and missiologists. Evangelists are reapers and often respond to urgency. Missiologists operate with wide angle lenses and sensitivity to cultures. Both are valid callings and represent two sides of the church's mission mandate, but in practice they often compete. The Lausanne Covenant of 1974, articulated by Billy Graham and John Stott but influenced powerfully by Latin and African voices, carefully sought to nuance these and other mission issues, and has guided much of my own mission theology ever since.

---

[27] To prepare for a discussion of these and other contemporary mission issues, see the writings of Andrew Walls, Phillip Jenkins, and Lamin Sanneh, *Disciples of All Nations: Pillars of World Christianity* (NY: Oxford Press, 2008).

106

CYRIL AND METHODIUS

OF MORAVIA

826 to 869

(869 for Cyril, 885, Methodius)

CYRIL AND METHODIUS
OF MORAVIA

Tensions between the Roman Catholic and Greek Orthodox churches had been growing, especially since 787 when the western church altered the Nicean Creed. It added the word *filioque*: "and the Son." To Greeks and other Orthodox, this was unthinkable. Other tensions happened along the northern and western borders after Pope Leo III crowned Charlemagne on Christmas Day 800, making him Holy Roman Emperor.

Charlemagne was in the process of conquering northern areas along the Danube and Moravian Rivers, thereby extending Catholic influence north and east, to the chagrin of Orthodox church leaders. By now Islam blocked the church from expanding south and east, but it could instead go north and west.

Bulgars had moved into the region. King Rostislav of Moravia begged the Greek Patriarch for a mission to the Slavic world and its many groups of peoples. King Boris the Bulgar was being courted for Roman baptism by Louis the German, who ruled east of the Rhine. The Pope in Rome wrote to him hoping a Catholic king would let Rome appoint a Catholic bishop. The Patriarch in Istanbul did the same thing, hoping for a Greek bishop. But Boris wanted to appoint his own national bishop and not be an appendage to either empire.

In Istanbul, two Thessalonian Greek-speaking brothers, Cyril and Methodius, were commissioned for a mission to the Slavs. Cyril, the primary translator, created a Slavic alphabet later known as Cyrillic. Methodius was primarily a preacher, but also an effective evangelist using biblical art. Between them they created a pan-Slavic literature. Their ecclesiastical work created a theological fault line in eastern Europe that has lasted into our own time. Serbs, Bulgarians, and Russians aligned with the Orthodox church, while the other northern Slavs, Croats, Slovenes, Czechs, Slovaks, and Poles united with the Roman Catholic church.

While it is getting ahead of the story chronologically, I will observe that many Slavs have found a way to observe both ecclesiastical traditions. They are called *Uniates* because they are Orthodox in worship and theology, but as a result of later events switched their governing allegiance to Rome. My own parish community in Chicago included the headquarters of the Ukranian Catholic Church: united with Rome in authority, but totally Orthodox in worship and theology. I got to know one scholar priest very well, and took visitors to those churches for many years. There are other *Uniate* churches such as the Maronite and Melkite churches in Lebanon and Israel, but they have different historical origins.

The translation mission of these Slavic brothers highlights a major difference between Christianity and Islam in mission approach. Both are committed to evangelism and actively seek converts by many means, both good and bad. Christianity translates the Bible and contextualizes the church into local cultures, while Islam imposes Arabic customs and language on local cultures, including teaching converts the Koran in Arabic. Professor Lamin Sanneh of Yale has written on this extensively in *Encountering the West: Christianity and the Global Cultural Process: The African Dimension.*[28]

---

[28] Maryknoll NY: Orbis Books, 1993.

110

In 1539 Luther wrote a wonderful essay, *On the Councils and the Church,* suggesting that the primary task of the church in every generation is to do a fresh inventory, and separate faith issues from cultural issues. The early church did this in the first Jerusalem Council.[29] First they defined the Gospel as Jesus pure and simple: who he was, what he did and continues to do. Jesus alone is the faith issue. Everything else is a cultural issue to be guided by the love principle in the Bible.

We all know that in the process of transmitting the faith, many cultural biases are shared, and many become intertwined with the Gospel, approaching canonical or official acceptance in later generations. These Slavic brothers did for Slavs what Dante did later for Italians and Luther did for Germans. They translated the Bible into the people's tongue. In so doing, they empowered local culture and created common languages. They trusted the Holy Spirit with the plain text.

They also paid a price. After Cyril died, Methodius was put into prison for three years. His crime: translating the Bible into Moravian. These were the same Moravians who later gave the world Hus of Prague, and Nicholas Count Zinzendorf of Moravia who influenced Wesley and the eighteenth century Lutheran Pietist missions to many nations.

These brothers remind us that mission is profoundly radical in the true sense of going to the roots *(radix).* This line, from the opponents of mission in Acts, describes Cyril and Methodius: "The people who have turned the world upside down have come hither also."[30]

---

[29] Acts 15

[30] Acts 17: 6

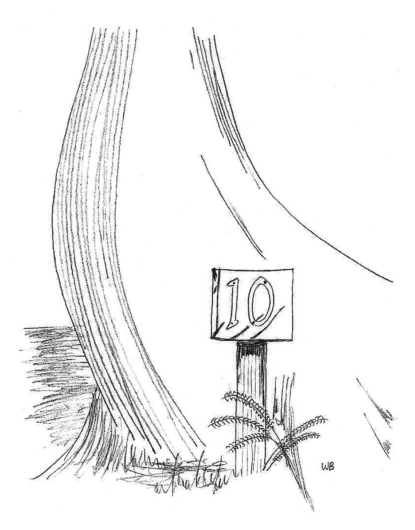

OLGA OF KIEV

879 to 969

Today, what we call Russia and Ukraine together make a patchwork quilt of many Slavic subcultures. One of the great *what ifs* of history relates to the question: what if Russia had become Muslim instead of Christian? Surely the history of Europe would have been very different. Knowledgeable historians attribute Orthodox Russia and Ukraine to the tenth century invasions by Swedes, first to trade and then to rule.

Swedish traders had discovered two rivers running north and south, one to the Black Sea and the other to the Caspian. With a base in the north, Viking King Ryunik occupied Kiev. Eventually his son Igor became king and married Olga, who, at Igor's death in 945, ruled Kiev for nineteen years. She was a professing Christian. In 957 she decided to visit Constantinople, to seek baptism by the Patriarch (which she did), hoping to strengthen her authority. When she returned and tried to establish Christianity, a rebellion broke out. Her son Sviatoslav took over the throne and, some say, considered becoming Muslim. No long-term religious commitments were made, as he was busy fighting wars on the western and eastern fronts. When he was killed in battle, Olga's grandson, Vladimir the 2nd, came to power and ruled from 980-1015.

Vladimir took the religious question seriously, needing a religion to unite his people. Bainton said Vladimir could never give up pork to be Jewish, or alcohol to be Muslim, although "he had no aversion to polygamy in Paradise." [31] More seriously, he also considered how much independence he would lose with the various religious

---

[31] Bainton, *Christendom*, p. 117.

options. One of the groups he sent out to explore experienced the glorious liturgy at Hagia Sophia in Constantinople. They returned promoting the Christian option. Latourette, for one, feels the story of groups sent to explore various faiths is a total fabrication, and so it may be. Olga would have joined in the option for Christianity, and perhaps she had assistance from Anna – Greek princess, Byzantine Christian, and member of Vladimir's array of wives – in influencing the decision. In 988 Vladimir commanded his army to ride their horses into the river for a mass baptism. Russia and Ukraine became Christian overnight. Shades of Queen Esther perhaps, when a little palace intrigue shapes history

This event turned the whole nation in a Greek direction. Simultaneously, a host of mission movements in Norway, Sweden, and Denmark moved all the Scandinavian countries into the Roman or Latin Church. Kiev became the ecclesiastical center for Russia until 1325 when the church capitol moved to Moscow.

The Russian Orthodox church in subsequent centuries evangelized in eleven time zones: from western Europe, across Asia and Alaska, finally ending up just north of San Francisco. Native churches were planted all along the way. It is a glorious story, told by Dr. Michael Oleksa in his dissertation titled *Alaska Missionary Spirituality*,[32] and later in his delightful book, *Orthodox Alaska: A Theology of Mission*.[33]

In 1983 I visited Anchorage and paid a call on Bishop Nicholas at the Russian Orthodox Cathedral. He graciously responded to my questions about the Russian church. I asked whether the hierarchy of the church had

---

[32] NY: Paulist Press, 1987.
[33] Crestwood NY: St. Vladimir's Seminary Press, 1992.

114

been compromised through actions of communist leaders like Lenin, Stalin, and their successors. He assured me that, indeed, church leaders had to make deals so the church could survive, "but not the babushka women!" He told me that the women are the strength of that church. Then, with gusto, he added: "In 1988 [five years hence], the whole world will know who the real Russians are. The Communists have been there seventy years. We will have been there a thousand years!"

In 1984, Billy Graham and I listened to each other as opening plenary speakers at the Urbana Mission Conference for students. Billy had just returned from his high profile visit to Russia and had dropped in at the White House for a private dinner with the Reagans before arriving at Urbana. I had the privilege of an evening meal with Billy and Gordon McDonald, the newly elected director of InterVarsity Christian Fellowship. Billy repeated to Gordon and to me what he had told the Reagans: "There is a revival of Christianity in Russia that is so deep and so wide, the communist leaders don't know what to do about it." The Politburo of leaders kept Billy for one hour and twenty minutes in a serious quest: "What does it mean?"

Sure enough, the wall came down in Berlin in 1989, thanks, I think, far more to the Orthodox prayers in the east, and a Polish Pope and a Polish Catholic Church organizing in the west, than to the triumph of western politicians and capitalism. But, sadly, rather than coming alongside those long oppressed Christians to ask how we might help them recover, western mission agencies flooded eastern Europe. Pastors reported going to the airports constantly to meet the latest delegations, all wanting to preach in Russian pulpits, and start projects they could take credit for when they returned home. It was so bad, I actually heard a few Cuban Christians say that they hope Castro lives forever, to prevent them being deluged by American Christians coming to save them.

To many in the west, I recommend *A Long Walk To Church: A Contemporary History of Russian Orthodoxy* by Nathaniel Davis.[34] It describes the systematic ways by which the communist government stripped the Orthodox church of its seminaries, hospitals, social ministries, and treasures, and closed so many congregations. It seemed you could go a thousand miles before you found another open church, and it functioned only under strict government supervision. Then, when this great church was so weak, the flood gates opened, compounding the struggle.

Of course we are not surprised, that as Orthodoxy now grows strong, it is retreating from collaboration with the west. That is tragic. The Orthodox churches remind me of the alpine trees that grow along the tree line at Mount Baker. They live most of the year under twenty feet of snow. They are bent, but they survive. During the brief summer they thrive, then go back under the snow for another winter. They do not produce great lumber like the Douglas fir that grows open, tall, and straight, but they survive and possess a beauty and integrity few trees can match. Western Christians are the descendents of Christians who came "yearning to breathe free." How quickly we have forgotten our heritage.

---

[34] Boulder, CO: Westview Press, 1995.

116

ANSELM OF CANTERBURY

1033 to 1109

ANSELM OF CANTERBURY

To those who know much about the history of mission, Anselm may seem like a strange choice for a mission trail. From 1093 until his death, he was Archbishop of Canterbury, but spent much of that time in exile from English kings who disputed the power and authority of official church leaders. While in exile he wrote books that made him famous among emerging academics in Europe.

By the year 1000 Europe had become Christian. In other words, Christendom was well established in all but the most remote areas. Seen more broadly from a church perspective, while Europe saw the rising influence of Christianity, historically Christian areas of Africa and Asia were declining, as Islam grew dominant. Wealth increased as Europe gradually turned from facing the Mediterranean to facing the Atlantic. Urban centers proliferated with prosperous merchant classes and the beginnings of new kinds of schools. In previous centuries, monastic schools had the advantage, but cities produced cathedrals. Cathedrals with powerful bishops began to create schools with subjects other than just theology and canon (church) law. Civil law, philosophy, medicine, and the arts emerged. Lay scholars, not just monks or abbots, were prepared to teach.

In 1066 William from France conquered England and brought his famous monastic scholar, LanFranc, from the abby at Bec to be Archbishop of Canterbury. LanFranc had been the teacher who most inspired Anselm, who then joined the monastery at Bec and began to flourish as an intellectual. At the death of LanFranc, many church leaders wanted Anselm to become Archbishop, but by then English kings were looking for ways to rid themselves of Roman authority. They preferred to have bishops accountable to a local monarch.

Hildebrand, elected Pope as Gregory VII in 1073, worked to bring major reforms to the Catholic church in Europe. Married priests and married monks often prospered, and at death handed off significant monastic or church properties to their sons, who, like Eli's sons in the Old Testament Samuel story, had their fathers' anointing but not necessarily Gods'. Out-of-control clergy sometimes sold church offices. Emerging kings wanted power to appoint bishops. It was a classic conflict as Europe began to experience the rise of political leaders in territories not yet become national states.

Gregory passed many reforms, but two were game-changers for Europe and the church. He required all priests and monks to be celibate. Until 1074, priests in the west, like Orthodox priests in the east, were married. Monks were celibate in both churches. Presumably, if priests could not marry, they would not have sons to inherit property. A second reform involved lay investiture or the idea that lay leaders would not have the right or power to appoint bishops. Only church leaders could *invest* or appoint bishops. Anselm's appointment to Archbishop of Canterbury meant that he would be called upon to enforce those new church laws in England.

Long before Henry VIII broke with the church, English kings were growing increasingly independent. It was only seventy years after Anselm that Thomas à Becket, the Archbishop, was assassinated in Canterbury Cathedral by henchmen of the King of England. When English King Henry appointed bishops in Anselm's absence, he refused to consecrate them at his return. That inflamed the king even more.

Today, as wealth and fame increases, it has become fashionable for evangelical leaders to hand off their churches, schools, foundations, and television empires to their sons. From what I am observing, some of the same troubles result. They also may have their daddy's call, but not the Lords'.

What makes Anselm a person of mission interest has less to do with his church struggles, and more to do with his scholarly writings, most of which took shape when he was in exile. Small universities – in their start-up phase – and many new students were questioning traditional Christian beliefs. In a real sense he is a founder of the Rene Descartes-thinking Christian tradition. In that sense I see him as a patron saint for campus ministers who are called upon to help make sense of faith in the context of universities, where doubt is the prevailing culture.

Anselm was one of the first to use reason, rather than biblical quotations, as a method of argument for belief in God. In his book *Fides Quaerens Intellectum* (Faith Seeking Understanding), he made famous the statement: "I believe in order to understand." In *Proslogian* (Disputes), he argued that God is "that-than-which-no-greater-can-be-thought." We cannot conceive of the non-existence of space and time, so, like God, they must exist necessarily and eternally.

He is equally famous for his idea about the atonement and incarnation in *Cur Deus Homo* (Why God Became Man). Contrary to many theologians since Irenaeus in the second century, Anselm did not see the atonement as Christ's triumph over evil, or an overcoming of the Devil, or, like his contemporary Abelard, as an overwhelming demonstration of God's love. He used the category of law to suggest that human sin had violated God's honor, and no human could ever satisfy the need to redeem God's honor. Jesus Christ, as God-become-man, could represent God to satisfy the violated honor that our sins had caused, and could represent humans in need of a savior. Christ is the substitute and pays our penalty. Those who accept Christ's righteousness as sufficient payment for their sins are forgiven, freed, and thus granted eternal life.[35]

It was never Anselm's idea to prove you could reason your way to faith without the Bible, but he clearly sought to explain his biblical faith in rational ways that emerging university students could appreciate. Whether you like or dislike his views on faith and reason, he is considered by many to have been the greatest theologian between Augustine and Thomas Aquinas. A devoted student of Augustine, he believed philosophy could be a helpful tool: an aid to faith, but not a substitute for faith.

---

[35] I recommend two basic collections of Anslem's writings: *The Library of Christian Classics,* Vol. X, *A Scholastic Miscellany: Anselm to Ockham.* ed. and trans. Eugene Fairweather (Philadelphia: Westminster Press, 1956), pp. 47-208; *Saint Anselm Basic Writings*, trans. S. N. Deanne (Chicago: Open Court Publishing, 1962).

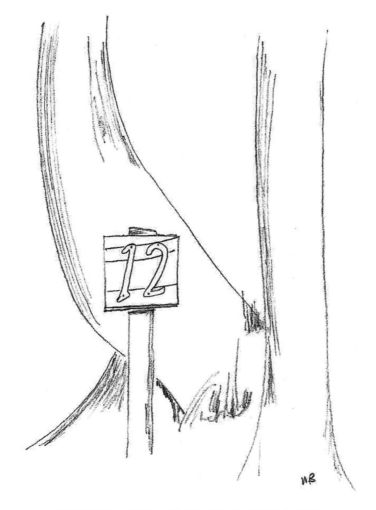

BERNARD OF CLAIRVAUX

1090 to 1153

BERNARD OF CLAIRVAUX

While Europe claimed to be Christian, it hardly looked like our idea of the Kingdom of God. Warring princes and factionalism prevailed in society, and rationalism had become commonplace in the newly emerging universities. When Bernard was but five years old, Pope Urban II called for a crusade to capture Jerusalem from the clutches of infidels (Muslims). He called it God's will that Turks be killed for the glory of God. European armies did succeed in taking Jerusalem, but that victory was but the tragic beginning of a centuries' old conflict that continues today. To make matters worse, the church hierarchy was in shambles. Church offices were for sale. Monasteries had declined. Others were sacked. Everywhere people craved reform.

Bernard had great intellectual capacities, but emerged as an even more powerful personality. That was apparent at age twenty-three when he showed up at the historic monastery of Citeaux, France, with thirty friends including his brothers, all asking to be admitted as monks. Two years later, at age twenty-five, he was asked to establish and become abbott for a new monastery at Clairvaux. Long before this, Cluny had been the center of Benedictine life, influence, and growing wealth. But their wealth became their undoing, and in the resulting spiritual vacuum, other new monasteries and movements came about, including the one at Citeaux. But when Bernard showed up, the order grew too fast! He not only created the house at Clairvaux, he influenced the building of an additional five hundred monastic houses that spread across Europe.

I sometimes explain the difference between Benedictines and Cistercians (as Bernard's followers were called) in this way. I call the Benedictines *Baptists* because they were autonomous, self ruled, and elected their own abbots. By contrast the Cistercians were like Presbyterians, connected to each other as though in a denomination. Connectedness enforced the discipline and rule, but united power became very seductive. When one of Bernard's students became Pope Eugenius and called for a second crusade, he asked Bernard to preach around Europe in order to raise support. By all accounts of his contemporaries, Bernard was the greatest preacher of the whole mediaeval era.

Unfortunately, the Crusade ended up as a total disaster, both for Europe and for Jerusalem. When Muslims saw Christians invading, they were ready. After defeating the Crusaders, they began systematic attacks on eastern Orthodox Christians: sacking monasteries, burning churches, and executing many Christian leaders. Western Catholics had finally split with Eastern Orthodoxy in 1054, but the gap had been widening for at least three centuries. Few who study the Crusades would disagree with me when I say that they went to conquer Islam, but in reality they ended up destroying the integrity and capacity of the eastern churches to sustain their leadership in the Middle East, North Africa, and the area from western Asia to India. The memory of Crusades continues to inflame Muslims today. They respond with Jihad. The Crusades empowered Islamic military leaders to gain huge influence. When the premier military leader, Salah ad Din (Saladin), consolidated power around the Middle East from his base in Egypt, he rivaled the leadership of the Caliph in Baghdad. That tension permeates Islamic societies in our own day. To some extent, it is the same tensions we see between popes and kings in so called Christian lands.

126

But Bernard was not primarily a politician. He was a mystic in love with Jesus, who sought to bring warmth and devotion to Jesus through popular Latin hymns still sung in our own time. Consider this verse from "O Sacred Head Now Wounded," attributed to Bernard of Clairvaux:

> What language shall I borrow,
>   to thank thee dearest friend,
> For this thy dying sorrow,
>   thy pity without end?
> O make me thine forever;
>   and should I fainting be,
> Lord, let me never, never,
>   outlive my love for thee.

He preached hundreds of sermons and wrote an amazing number of tracts that circulated all over Europe. He used the Mary and Martha story in the gospels to show that the contemplative life of Mary is preferred; but if we, like Martha, find traditional work and service to be our lot, we must bear it with patience. He was strongly orthodox yet he brought a much stronger devotion to Mary than was normal in that time. But he did not accept her Immaculate Conception, believing that only Christ was without sin. I find it humorous that he loved to preach sermons on the Song of Solomon to cloistered nuns in convents around Europe. The late Methodist historian William R. Cannon describes that when Bernard began quoting the biblical text, "Let him kiss me with the kisses of his mouth," he could hear "audible gasps of love-starved nuns all the way from the balcony."[36]

---

[36] Bainton, *Christendom*, p. 194 speaks of these sermons from Song of Solomon. I cannot find the source of the quote by Bill Cannon.

While his mission impact was huge for both good and ill, Bernard is, for me, also a reminder that spiritual power and influence can be overwhelmingly seductive to political leaders of the age. Many Christians I admire, and to whom I owe much, have been targeted for their audiences, such as Billy Graham, who later admitted he was "taken in" by Nixon. I watched Latin American junta-led generals reach out to Evangelical and Pentecostal pastors and evangelists when Catholic leaders sided with the poor and oppressed. When marginalized minority Christians, often derided as fundamentalists, finally get government leaders to welcome them, it feels so good for a change, like a blessing from God. We hear that some businesses are too big to fail, and it is obvious to all that they get special treatment from our political leaders. Huge ministries gain special favors as well, all done in the name of the one born in a stable, who lived among and cared for the poor and needy, and called us to follow him.

I so appreciate Bernard. I just hate to see him get used. The gifts and anointing of leaders make them attractive to those who need their help. St. Bernard, Billy Graham, and John Paul II have what today we call *soft power*. This is God-given influence. It must be stewarded well. We all benefit when that happens. From Augustine to the present, we know that *common grace* comes to societies when leaders are just and competent. It is a supreme task for Christian leaders to use their influence, when possible, to promote social good. But everyone is benefited by leaders who know where their calling and allegiance lies, and the difference between honor due their nation and primary allegiance to the values of the Kingdom of God.

FRANCIS OF ASSISI

1181 to 1226

FRANCIS OF ASSISI

Francis Bernardone was the son of a wealthy Italian merchant, who expected his son to honor his father, his position in the town, and multiply his wealth and influence. Francis seems to have enjoyed a frivolous youth, and when Assisi made war with neighboring Perugia, Francis put on knight's armor complete with a plumed helmet and went to war. Captured in battle, he became a prisoner for one year. After his release, he was very ill for a time.

While riding one day, he encountered a leper on the road who seemed to have the face of Christ. He dismounted, kissed him, placed him on his horse and led him to town. That was the beginning. He soon had visions that he should rebuild the old parish church in Assisi that had fallen into ruin. He ended up giving all his wealth and persuaded others to join the project. His father locked him in the cellar and appealed to city fathers to do something. The bishop decreed that if Francis would not care wisely for his inheritance, he should give it up. This he did, apparently stripping naked in the streets before his father, who was taking credit for the clothes on his back. In 1208 he left for the woods to live the life of a hermit. Soon others joined him to form a community. Two years later they went to Rome to ask Pope Innocent III for recognition. He told them they could be *Friars Minor* and continue penitential preaching, but withheld formal recognition. A soul sister, Clare, came along to found the order of Poor Clares. Frances went about Europe singing, preaching, begging, and giving to the poor wherever he went.

Possessed of a missionary spirit, Francis decided in 1212 he should be a missionary in Syria. He started out, but failed to complete the journey, prevented by misfortune aboard ship. He attempted another trip through Spain to North Africa, but did not complete that journey either. Back in Italy, he appealed to the Fourth Lateran Council in 1215 for recognition, but without success. In 1219 he journeyed to Egypt and preached to the Sultan, who did not convert. In 1220 he bowed in obedience before his successor and retired to a life of solitude and devotion. Finally in 1223, the new Pope Honorius III officially recognized the Friars Minor. Francis' rules, so very strict, were relaxed. At his death in the chapel of Assisi in 1226, his order had become a powerful spiritual force in Europe.

In contrast to Francis, who was so intentionally poor that he did not own a Psalter, Dominic, a brilliant scholar born in Spain a few years before Francis, came to the same Pope Innocent III to ask permission to found an order to train preachers to preach the great theological themes of Scripture. He was not given an independent order, so he adapted the Canons of Saint Augustine and formed an Order of Preachers. Whereas Francis drew his followers from the poor, Dominic drew his preachers from the educated upper classes. However, his ministry confronted him with the Albigensians, a group that took the Gospel and poverty seriously and fled to the mountains in southern France. Dominic realized that the attraction of this group was the radical commitment of its leaders to poverty and an ascetic life style, very different from the church leaders of the time. Like Francis, he insisted his order become *Mendicant* (a begging order).

Dominic's order began to confront the heresies of the time with great scholarship, writing, and preaching. His best student, Thomas Aquinas, arrived early in the movement. They believed the best antidote to heresy was to become well-armed students of Orthodox Christianity. They tried with limited success to convert Jews and Moslems as well. It was not long before the Dominicans had placed their scholars in faculties around Europe. Quite surprisingly, in time, the Franciscans also produced scholars, most notably Alexander of Hales, who became their first university professor.

Francis had been interested in missions, and one of his followers, John of Montecorvino, visited Persia, Ethiopia, India, and finally the city we know today as Beijing, China. Within a few years he had made thousands of converts.

After Francis died, his order split between the rigorous and the modernists, my names for them. Pope Gregory IX, in 2030, declared Francis' Rule non-binding. By 2045 the Franciscans began to own property, and eventually universities as well. Almost from the start, their history was more tumultuous than the Dominicans.

For me, Francis and Dominic represent two sides of the great commandment of Jesus as recorded in Matthew.[37] Dominic sought permission to found an order to train great scholars and preachers who would love God with all their heart, mind, soul, and strength. He epitomizes the first commandment.

By contrast, Francis sought an order that could take the Gospel to the streets, and love the poor and downtrodden as much as he loved himself. Taken together, they are two sides of the ministry coin as it were, and together they provided renewal to the Catholic church for more than seven centuries. If Francis and Dominic had been

---

[37] Matthew 22:36-40

Protestant or Evangelical, I suspect they would have founded separate and rival denominations.

But I do see a need to keep Dominic and Francis together if our spirituality is to be vibrant and sustainable for the journey. The civil rights movement began with a biblical justice passion, but within a generation the piety of the movement slid into public moralism. Equally sad is what happened to Luther and Calvin's reform movements, which in less than a century had descended into barren scholasticism.

The Great Awakening in the colonies (from 1740s), led for two decades by mental and spiritual giants like Jonathan Edwards and George Whitfield, modeled a piety that transformed society in thirteen independent colonies, and led to the founding of many new colleges. But gradually that piety also turned to moralism, and by 1776 only about ten percent of the people bothered to attend churches. The revivals of the Second Awakening (after 1800), led to massive social reforms, frontier and overseas missions. Evangelism became a studied technique for some. In revivalism, one needed only enough gospel to get saved.

There were exceptions of course, but my own experience of watching city ministries start well and flame out or gradually die, lead me to conclude that for any ministry to be sustained long-term, the Francis of Assisi and Mother Teresa types need the Dominics and tools of biblical scholarship.

I have been impressed with the vitality of the Coptic Orthodox church. It is surviving, even thriving, under pressure. All city pastors spend at least one month a year in a monastery for continued study, contemplation, worship, and spiritual renewal. Pope Shenuda and the bishops are brilliantly educated. Many, like the Pope, have doctorates, but they balance scholarship with incredible pastoral care and outreach in their parishes among the poor and marginalized. Or, as I say, "they keep Francis and Dominic together."

RAYMOND LULL OF MAJORCA

1232 to 1315

RAYMOND LULL OF MAJORCA

slam continued advancing westward through Europe until the year 732, when it was stopped at Tours, France, just outside Paris, by Charles Martel, king of the Franks. Spain then launched what would become a seven hundred year crusade to push Moors – African Muslims – out of Spain and Portugal and back into North Africa. But not every Christian in Europe believed that crusades or violence was the appropriate way to treat Muslims. Winning territory by violence is not true mission in any biblical sense.

Lull was born on Majorca, off the coast of Spain, shortly after Muslims were banished. He grew up with wealth and political connections. He married, but led a frivolous life until he began seeing repeated visions of Christ on the Cross. In 1263 he committed his life to Christ and began to think about missions, especially to Muslims.

Though he had relationships with both Franciscans and Dominicans, he was a mystic and too independent to fit into communal monastic life. He sold his properties to create enough wealth to support his wife and child, and set out to learn Arabic. He persuaded the king to help him create a school on the island to train missionaries for a mission in Arabic culture and language. His study became a nine-year ordeal of personal trauma. He purchased a Saracen slave to teach him Arabic. To this slave he practiced his message. The frustrated slave responded angrily to being hit by Lull, and struck back with a weapon that inflicted a deep wound. Jailed and in remorse, the slave committed suicide. Lull took time to recover, but then received a fresh vision of his call: to treat Muslims with love and not hate. He traveled widely and developed a philosophical apologetic that he felt would be sensitive and effective for presenting the Gospel to Arabs in North Africa.

He visited the Pope to secure his support. More than once Lull lectured in the universities of Paris and Montpelier, engaging the best theological scholarship of the day. Finally he presented his plan to the Dominicans, who were not interested, and then to the Franciscans, who were. He also preached in synagogues and mosques around Europe, and finally left for Africa with his three-pronged strategy: education, apologetics, and evangelism. He wrote over sixty books on theology in his lifetime, mostly aimed at Muslim intellectuals.

Probably the person who did the most to revive Lull's legacy was another great scholar and missionary to Muslims, Samuel Zwemer (1867-1952), who founded and edited *The Muslim World* journal for thirty-five years and taught at Princeton Seminary from 1929 to 1937. He wrote *Raymond Lull: First Missionary to Moslems.*[38]

Largely through Lull's influence, the great universities at Paris, Oxford, Salamanca, and Bologna added Hebrew, Arabic, and Chaldean (Syriac) languages to their curriculum. At age eighty, he returned one last time to Africa. He spent some months in secret, counseling converts, but finally went public and told the crowd that he was the person they had expelled forty years before. In a fury, on 30 June 1315, they stoned him outside the city. Followers brought his body back to Palma, Majorca, where his tomb can be visited today.

---

[38] NY: Funk and Wagnalls, 1902.

Lull was not the first scholar to advocate the study of Hebrew, Greek, Arabic, and Syriac for theological purposes. Stephen Neill, another great mission scholar, noted that Lull was the first person to believe that learning those languages was the key to effective evangelism. Lull himself believed that missionaries will convert the world by preaching, shedding of tears and blood, hard labor, and martyrdom. From a review of his last mission trip into North Africa we learn that contemporaries described him as confrontational and unstable. However, it is hard for me to imagine greater contrasts than existed between the crusader approach and Lull's lifetime of study, love, and passion for the people he wanted to hear and understand the Trinity and God's love.

When I first created the mission trail in 1995 and until this writing, I used another name to represent the fourteenth century of mission: John Wyclif of Oxford (1329-1384). He has been called *the morning star of the Reformation*, because he anticipated many of Luther's ideas in his own passion to translate the Bible into the English language. He trained followers called Lollards, and sent them all over England to share the biblical Gospel. He lived during the Hundred Years War between France and England, a horribly brutal time when one third of Europe died in three years from the Great Plague, when the Baltic Sea was so cold it froze over three winters in a row, and when rival Catholic popes lived in Avignon, France. Amazing ministry occurred during those years. Wyclif was at the center of much that we need to know and celebrate, especially those many anonymous pastors whose ministry involved collecting infected bodies for burial, deliberately assuring their own miserable deaths, but with no one left to remember their martyrdom. To get insight into this period, I recommend Barbara Tuchman's reconstruction of the period in her book, *A Distant Mirror: The Calamitous 14th Century*.[39]

Unfortunately the image of Dark Ages or Middle Ages conjures up in our minds the idea that for one thousand years nothing much or good happened. The darkness is probably in our minds because of the historical bias in evangelical Protestantism: that between the New Testament and the Reformation, nothing of importance to our theology or witness can be learned. Nothing is further from the truth.

The Reformation was not a clean break from the past. I agree with scholar Heiko Augustinus Oberman that the Reformation is a flowering of what was happening for at least three hundred years.[40] Luther was doubtless more medieval than modern in his ideas and scholarship, but that is not to deny the value of the Reformation or renewal of churches in the sixteenth century. It is recognition that the Holy Spirit was teaching the church new ways to be pastors, missionaries, and lay folk in the market place. To ignore that, I think, is a not-so-subtle way of blaspheming the Holy Spirit, whose gift from the beginning has been to teach the church.

I acknowledge this when I call myself a "historical charismatic." It also reminds me, as a contemporary Baptist, that my brand of Christianity has roots that go deeply into all the Catholic and Orthodox traditions of theology, ministry, and pastoral care. At the very least, we should breath a prayer of thanks for those churches whenever we pass by their facilities in our cities. Better

---

[39] NY: Alfred A. Knopf, 1978.

[40] *The Dawn of the Reformation: Essays in Late Medieval and Early Reformation Thought* (Edinburgh: T. & T. Clark LTD., 1986).

140

yet, as I learned long ago, why not stop and thank those priests for the centuries of faithfulness to God before we existed?

HUS OF PRAGUE

1373 to 1415

HUS OF PRAGUE

On a hot summer day in 1968, I was invited to preach at both morning and evening services in Marengo, Illinois, about seventy-five miles northwest of Chicago. Because I had no cash to take the toll-way, I drove old route 12. After the morning service everyone left, with no one inquiring about my plans. As I had neither money nor credit cards, lunch was out of the question. Instead, I found a cemetery with a single shade tree next to a grave marked Smith, where I sat and read *Advocates of Reform: From Wyclif to Erasmus*, Volume XIV in my *Library of Christian Classics*. That hot afternoon, I discovered an amazing essay by John Hus: "On Simony." A few hours later I returned to the little Baptist church to preach in the evening service, and was told they would send a check later. I drove the slow road back to Chicago, arriving very late. It was a great day for I truly fell in love with the advocates of church reform in the fourteenth and fifteenth centuries, and all the ways they sought to implement their ideas. I have lectured many times since on the subject.

John Hus is another person whom we do not generally think belongs on a mission trail, perhaps instead on a ministry trail. He did not go far from home, but his burning at the stake at the Council of Constance (1415) inflamed movements that resulted in "the flowering of lay piety," a description used by Latourette. Beginning in Bohemia and Moravia (Czech and Slovak Republics), bretheran movements began taking root in Europe and eventually included Moravians and Mennonites. This lay movement had an incredible influence on spreading mission activity all over the world and into our present era.

Born of poor parents who wanted him to be a priest, Hus began primary school at age thirteen and continued until he completed his BA and MA at the University of Prague. By 1396 he had begun to teach there in the faculty of arts, and soon became a popular preacher at Bethlehem Church, near the campus at city center.

Many Czech students went to England to study (after the king's daughter married King Richard II of England), and they got hold of Wyclif's writings. Those writings began finding their way to Prague and Hus' attention. The Archbishop of Prague banned them, but the Prague university faculty unanimously committed to study them.

Hus was not as radical as Wyclif, but he had strong convictions on some key points. He believed that Christ was head of the church, not popes. At that time of rival popes, such a view was more palatable. He also believed that laity should receive the cup of wine at communion, not just the clergy. The church had long taught that lay folk ought not to partake for fear of spilling the blood of Christ. Laity were often much more devout than their clergy. That teaching represented the growing gulf between clergy and laity.

The Emperor called the Council of Pisa in 1409 to depose the two rival popes, but a second council, Council of Constance in 1415, was needed to settle the papal question. At that time the church condemned the views of Wyclif and burned John Hus,[41] throwing his ashes into the lake so there would not be a shrine to foment more trouble in Bohemia. It did not work. Instead, church leaders lit a flame they could not put out. Calls for popular preaching and reform of clerical life-styles accelerated. The *Unitas*

---

[41] Hus means *goose* in Czech. The joke was they cooked his goose.

Fratrum (Moravian Brethren), with lay-driven communal piety and radical peace positions, emerged after a series of local civil wars.

Everyone agreed that reform was necessary, but how would it come about? In my own study of the question, I think we can summarize six of the most common approaches to reform of both church and society.

- Evangelism. The assumption in this model is that one-by-one conversion of individuals is the primary way to bring about reform. It is a time-honored approach, from sixteenth century preachers such as Wyclif, Hus, and Savanarola of Florence, to Billy Graham.

- Education. This approach originated with Erasmus of Rotterdam who assumed that knowledge leads to behavioral reform in church and society, especially education of the clergy. Erasmus led the *back to the Bible movement*, by producing the first Greek New Testament in 1516. He knew there were priests who had never seen a Bible, let alone know how to use one. From Erasmus to my own seminaries, where I studied and where I now teach, many believe this is basic to bringing reform.

- Government. This approach assumes that the church needs help. Henry VIII in England said: "Let Parliament reform the Church." Cardinal Ximenez in Spain said: "Let the Inquisition reform the Church." Both assumed the church is weak and needs outside government assistance, assumptions shared in our own time. Martin Luther King, Jerry Falwell, and James Dobson all lobbied government to assist the church in changing society.

- Councils. This assumption, if I can be direct, is that too much corruption resides with leadership at the top and, like manure, it needs to be spread out, since all know that it cannot be eliminated altogether. John Gerson, Peter D'Ailly, and Henry of Langenstein were among those who felt that if they could just get disputing parties together in councils, reforms would come. I think of these folk as the Peter Druckers of their time. They assume that with better management, goals, and respected lines of authority, reform can come. Who of us today have not been to courses or conferences to learn better the management of the church that will hopefully result in transformations of persons and society.

- New Testament Churches. The assumption is that existing churches are incapable of reform and we need to plant new churches that truly replicate New Testament standards. From people like Blaurock, Marpeck, and Menno Simons to church planting movements today, we hear repetitions of similar themes.

- Mission. The assumption here is that when the church is turned in upon itself in a satisfied, self-protecting mode, reform happens by reaching out. This idea is most singularly identified with Ignatius Loyola and the Jesuits, founded in 1540. Jesuits became one of the pillars of Pope Paul III's reforms followed the Council of Trent (1546-1553). When a whole new world opened up after Columbus, the Roman church became energized to explore and evangelize. Missional theology is in vogue everywhere today, but it too has ancient roots.

146

Since becoming aware that we all need each other and that no one reforming model alone will truly reform the church and society, I have consciously tried to incorporate most of these models on my own ministry journey.

LAS CASAS OF SPAIN

1474 to 1566

My inner city Chicago church had begun to incubate Spanish language churches before I arrived as pastor in 1969. By 1973, in partnership with the denomination, we had helped start five. I then began working with a small committee to start Seminario Biblico Hispano, a Spanish language Bible School that still carries on in Chicago. I had not prepared to work in the Spanish community or language, so I took a plunge into libraries and some brief language study. In that research I found a book with the intriguing title *Aristotle and the American Indians: A Study in Race Prejudice in the Modern World.*[42] It introduced me to the over half-century-long debate by Las Casas and Sepulveda in the courts of Spain before Kings Charles V and Phillip II. The debate focused on the new Natives under Spanish rule. Did they have souls? Sepulveda had translated Aristotle and agreed with him that some people were "natural born slaves." They need not be evangelized, but ruled through the sacraments and church-led communal structures called *encomiendas.*

I began to feel a little sorry for the two Spanish kings who doubled as emperors of the Holy Roman Empire, which included most of Europe. They had Lutheran battles in the north, Anglican separation in England, Muslim Turks knocking on the gates of Vienna, continuing corruption surrounding the papacy, and now this: a debate on how the new Indians should be treated in the West Indies, Mexico, Central and South America. On the one side were the

---

[42] Lewis Hanke (Bloomington, IN: Indiana University Press, 1959).

exploiters who coveted thc land and the gold; and on the other side were most of the missionaries, including Bartolome De Las Casas, the chief spokesman in what became a titanic justice struggle with consequences that continue today in all of those countries.

Shortly after finding Hanke's research, I encountered *The Other Spanish Christ* by John McKay, former president of Princeton Seminary after years of education and ministry in South America. His thesis was that the *conquestadors* (exploiters) permitted only two images of Christ to be shared with the Indians: the helpless baby in the mother's arms, and the emaciated Jesus on the Cross. Those two images would evoke powerful devotion, but avoid empowerment leading to social change and justice. It became obvious to me why liberation theology was not a threat to Jesus Christ, the Bible, or the true church, but rather a Latin gift to the church world wide: because it challenged Aristotilian structures of oppression imposed on Latin American peoples. Not surprisingly, the definitive work on Las Casas came from Gustavo Gutierrez: *Las Casas: In Search of the Poor of Jesus Christ.*[43]

Las Casas was not an early convert to the cause. A graduate in law at Salamanca, he had his own *encomienda*. Natives were not to be slaves, but they were often put in the care or trust of those who abused them. In 1521, when Indians revolted against a church-controlled settlement he and his colleagues had set up as a supposedly peaceful model in Venezuela, he withdrew and joined the Dominican Order. After that he intervened dramatically on the side of the Indians, offending most colonial leaders. In 1544, he secured new laws and treatment policies, but colonial leaders balked at the enforcement, even in his

---

[43] Maryknoll, NY: Orbis, 1992.

own diocese in Chiapas, Mexico, where he was installed as bishop at age seventy. Sadly, some of his own priests defied him, so he moved back to Spain for good.

All in all, he made four trips across the Atlantic, worked in Hispaniola (Cuba), traveled widely to promote just treatment of Indians, and participated in debates with Sepulveda and the King in 1850-51. He created a stir wherever he went. His books were banned in Peru during his lifetime. He spent his last years in Spain writing and speaking out until his death at age ninety-two. Some called him the *Apostle of the Indies*. Farmers vilified and blamed him for the decline in their profits. By the middle of the following century, all his books were on the Inquisition's list of forbidden books.

While every city in the new world had its churches and missions, there was no honest attempt to build up an indigenous church. Priests from Spain lived well in the new world, with hosts of Indians to wait on them. They showed almost no interest in evangelizing Indians in the interiors of their countries. Luis Rivera described Latin American evangelization as a "violent evangelism," both for the colonial methods Las Casas had opposed, but also because missionaries brought new diseases with them for which there were no immunities. Whole peoples and islands were decimated, an arrival consequence of those who came to bring a new faith in exchange for land and gold.[44]

The United States is now the second largest Spanish-speaking nation in the world. We recently passed Spain. Only Mexico, of the twenty-five Spanish-speaking

---

[44] Luis N. Rivera, *A Violent Evangelism: The Political and Religious Conquest of the Americas* (Louisville KY: Westminster/John Knox Press, 1990).

countries in South and Central America, has a larger population. Just before I left Chicago in 2000, that city welcomed its new Cardinal, Francis George. We learned that Cardinal George spoke perfect Spanish. When asked where he learned the language he replied, "When I was Bishop of Yakima." That city in Washington State has a Spanish-speaking majority. My research on Anchorage, Alaska, in the mid 1990's, revealed that the fastest growing group in that city was Mexican. In my view, it is critical that we study the history of our newest neighbors, and our complicity with their colonial oppression.

Psalm 24 reminds us that "the earth is the Lords." It seems that the Lord is bringing great numbers, and many Americans are in a panic. What surprises me is the visceral opposition to and fear of the increasing refugees in our midst. For centuries we have been a moated nation, preserving a myth that the world is predominantly white. It turns out that eighty-seven percent of God's earth is comprised of peoples of color. The so called *browning of America* is not good news to some white folks, who are inclined to retreat further into gated communities and a walled country.

In my view, US policies toward our hemispheric neighbors since the Monroe Doctrine of 1820, and our Cuban policy the past fifty years, are among the biggest reasons why they come.[45] It would cost less to work for a Latin American Common Market than to build gigantic walls between our countries, and to imprison or deport people who want jobs Americans are unwilling to perform. For Christians, many texts of Scripture require us to treat

---

[45] For a discussion of the seven streams of Latino migration into the US at this time and why they come, see Juan González, *Harvest of Empire: A History of Latinos in America* (NY: Penguin, 2000).

152

strangers and aliens as brothers, and welcome them as Ruth the Moabite was welcomed in Bethlehem, and as Jesus the undocumented refugee was welcomed in Egypt.

At the 16th stake on the mission trail at Bakken, when time and weather permits, our groups pause at the outdoor split-log chapel to reflect on God's mission and our own call. Many expect Luther might represent the sixteenth century, but he, Calvin, and other reformers were busy grappling with ecclesiastical issues. Protestant missions appeared later.

SPENER OF GERMANY

1605 to 1705

Phillip Jakob Spener was born into a devout
Protestant family in Alsace the same year that John
Arndt published his influential book, *True Christianity*.[46]
At Strasbourg, Phillip studied theology, history, and
philosophy under strict Lutheran direction (1651-1659).
Then he moved about Basle, Geneva, Stuttgart, and
Tubingen, and during those two years became fascinated
by preaching that called for repentance and regeneration.
In 1663 he received a preaching appointment in Strasbourg
and chose to complete his doctorate at the university.

Scholars who write on Pietism, like my friend Dale
Brown, always point to the devastating situation in
Germany following The Thirty Years War (1618-1648), in
which the population went from sixteen to six million.
Many were killed and perhaps more became refugees.
Brown writes: "The war was religiously divisive, morally
subversive, economically destructive, socially degrading,
and ultimately futile in its results."[47] If you did not share
the religion of your prince, you could either convert or
move to where a prince held your church's faith.

Catholics were quick to point out that Germany was
experiencing God's judgment for the Reformation, which
dated from one hundred years before. Spener disagreed.
He felt Luther's reforms were incomplete, that
sanctification needed to be added. At age thirty-one, when

---

[46] John Arndt, *True Christianity,* trans. Peter C. Erb (NY:
Paulist Press, 1979).
[47] *Understanding Pietism* (Grand Rapids MI: Eerdmans,
1978), p. 21.

Spener was assigned to supervise some regional pastors, he was appalled at their lack of biblical knowledge and religious convictions. He began to teach books of the Bible and call for times of prayer. Then in 1574 he was invited to write an introduction to a new edition of John Arndt's book. His essay, titled *"Pia Desideria"* (Pius Desires), became a standard for the Pietist movement. Spener appealed for six requirements to bring back the Reformation:

- The Word of God must be read well in public, and it must be studied, even in families, and groups, with all members invited to interpret.

- The spiritual priesthood must be restored, so that all Christians are ministering to, with, and for one another. The mutual cure of souls was a favorite topic, and a threatening one to some pastors.

- All Christians should be known by their deeds of alms and care for neighbors, and not just for what they believe. There will be a bias on putting faith into action.

- Controversies and disputes are to be avoided if at all possible, and those in error should be met with heartfelt love.

- Clergy education should include knowledge, but with a focus on truth that penetrates the soul. He favored books that edified.

- Preaching should be reformed as to be truly edifying. It should awaken faith and urge the fruits of faith, not merely parade the ostentatious learning of the preacher.[48]

Spener had the idea of putting lay people into small groups for Bible study and prayer, believing in what today we call the *bottom up approach* to renewal, where hosts of multiplied and empowered cells, over time, create renewal of large churches.

Critics of Pietism often lament the excesses of individualism and mysticism, situations where personal experience takes precedence over creeds, and where the introduction of a universal spiritual church with Christ as head diminishes the local congregations. Lay folk insulted some clergy by questioning whether they had ever had the experience of *weidergeburt* (the new birth). Other clergy learned that *Gottseligkeit* (godliness standards) could divide congregations. While some followers took pietistic ideas to extremes, it was not so of Spener. He sought to add a warm heart to the transformed mind in what, today, we would call a wholistic approach.

His movement, led by Francke, gained traction, and under Zinzendorf influenced missions first in Europe and then around the world. People like Wesley came to drink deeply of the pietist experience. He took that small cell covenant group with the warm heart theology into his lifelong quest to renew Anglicanism in the UK and beyond. Halle became a center of pietist mission that spread to Scandinavia.

---

[48] These are my summaries from Spener's *Pia Desideria,* Part III: "Proposals to Correct Conditions in the Church," pp. 87-122. What began as an essay by Spener, became a separate book. My English copy was translated by Theodore G. Tappert (Philadelphia: Fortress Press, 1964).

I often suggest that this 17th stake gives me one more opportunity to thank God for the sturdy lay-led Norwegian Lutheranism of Hans Nielson Hauge, who went up fjords and valleys all over Norway during the early 1800's when Napoleon was terrorizing much of Europe. The state church and government-paid clergy often had Hauge arrested, but he was irrepressible. Later Carl Olaf Rosinius came over the mountains from Sweden to fan the revival flames of the prayer house movements. Lutheran pietism, as I experienced it transplanted to this valley, was a beautiful blend of strong biblical authority, the Apostles Creed, and a love ethic for all neighbors, Christian and non-Christian, as we shared farm equipment and farm labor. Foreign mission was honored, but we were spared the toxic fundamentalism – we saw around us in many places – by a sturdy faith and simple creed: love God and neighbor and serve the world.

Contemporary historian Ruth Tucker has reminded us that one reason the Pietists could go so quickly and so far into foreign mission callings, was that they were largely from the artisan class. Wherever they went, they took their skills with them. They worked to support themselves and the charitable activities they organized. It seems they practiced *business as mission* before anyone had invented the now popular term.

Puritanism and Pietism were simultaneous renewal movements: Puritanism trying to de-Romanize English Anglicanism; and Pietism trying to add sanctification and personal spirituality within German Lutheranism. There were differences however. Puritanism took a top-down approach, starting with brilliantly educated clergy who would be well taught in the three languages of the Cross:

158

Hebrew, Greek, and Latin. Puritanism produced Jonathan Edwards and Princeton traditions in America.[49]

Pietism produced the bottom-up lay approach. It began as an outgrowth of inner mission movements in Scandinavia, where Lutheranism was organized with the Episcopal model, including government-certified churches with official clergy.[50]

After the Reformation, the Jansenism Movement formed to bring a more personal faith into parish life within the Catholic church. The Hasidic Movement does this with Judaism. Sufism continues to add a personal and mystical prayer tradition in Islam. Pascal is famous for his image of the heart as a vacuum or craving. There can be no denying that Pietism, in Germany first and then worldwide, has been a major influence in global mission. It turns out that transformed people transform churches that often transform societies.

---

[49] See the brilliant study by George M. Marsden, *Jonathan Edwards: A Life* (New Haven CT: Yale University Press, 2003).
[50] For a readable introduction to the similarities between English Puritism and German Pietism see John T. McNeill, *Modern Christian Movements* (NY: Harper, 1954).
\

DAVID GEORGE AND

GEORGE LIELE OF AMERICA

1742 to 1810 and 1752 to 1825

DAVID GEORGE AND

GEORGE LIELE OF AMERICA

I believe it was June 1980 when, as I entered the annual gathering of the American Missiological Society and Professors of Mission, Orlando Costas, my former seminary classmate and professor at Eastern Seminary, called to me: "Ray, come meet Pearl McNeill!" This elegant silver-haired professor taught missions at Virginia Union University, one of the American Baptist Denomination's historic African American schools. "Tell Ray what you've been studying," he continued. "George Liele," she responded quietly. I paused and then asked her forgiveness for not knowing about him. "No one does, and that is why I've spent my life researching David George and George Liele. They were the first foreign missionaries ever sent from America."

That was embarrassing! It was also a bombshell. All of us American Baptists know that the Judsons from Massachusetts were the first missionaries to be sent from the US, first by Congregationalists to India, and later by Baptists to Burma. We all know that the American Baptists Convention was the only major denomination specifically created to support a foreign mission. But it was not true. Pearl McNeill was right. The truth is that more than twenty years earlier, African American Baptists of Silver Bluff, South Carolina, and Savannah, Georgia, sent the first foreign missionaries.

I looked through great scholarly dictionaries in my library, published in the US and UK. I checked the gurus of mission – Walker, Latourette, Bainton, Neill, and Tucker – whose works were published primarily in the late 70's and early 80's. None mentions this information. I looked in another direction and found standard black church studies in my own library. Carter G. Woodson knew these facts when he first authored *The History of the Negro Church* in the 1920's.[51] Leroy Fitts included George and Liele in *A History of Black Baptists* in 1985.[52] Albert J. Raboteau included this information in *Slave Religion,* published in 1978.[53] James M. Washington included it in *Frustrated Fellowship* published in 1986.[54] Milton C. Sernett includes this story through letters in *Afro-American Religious History.*[55] *African American Religious Studies*, edited by Gayrud S. Wilmore, reports it.[56] InterVarsity Press seems to be the first evangelical publisher to do so, in *Dictionary of American Christianity,*[57] and says of Leile: "In 1784 he obtained permission (from the British) to preach in Jamaica, becoming the first African-American foreign missionary." Finally, in 1995 Eerdmans published a new standard evangelical comprehensive Christian history of the United States and Canada. Written by Mark

---

[51] *The History of the Negro Church* (1921; reprint, Washington DC: Associated Publishers, 1970).
[52] Nashville, TN: Broadman Press.
[53] *Slave Religion: The "Invisible Institution" in the Antebellum South* (NY: Oxford, 1978).
[54] *Frustrated Fellowship: The Black Baptist Quest for Social Power* (Macon, GA: Mercer University Press).
[55] *Afro-American Religious History: A Documentary Witness*, ed. Milton C. Sernett (Durnham, NC: Duke University Press, 1985).
[56] *African American Religious Studies: An Interdisciplinary Anthology* (Durham, NC: Duke University Press, 1989).
[57] Downers Grove IL: InterVarsity Press, 1990.

162

A. Noll, it includes three pages on David George and George Liele.[58]

By now you have learned that I have profound respect for the true historians who spend their lives in dusty archives searching through scraps of paper, and dating writings by learning to read water marks. Tom Schaffer, my McCormick colleague, did that for many years in the Yale library, trying to establish dates for Jonathan Edward's sermons, enabling a scholar like George Marsden, who came later, to study the theological and pastoral development of Edwards and write a definitive scholarly history. Finally, users of that history, like me, can interpret and teach with clarity and significance.

But I hope you also know by now that a point of view is a view from a point. While the fixed social class or theological bias of writers is well known, our discipline of history and church history is changing. I no longer say that Columbus discovered America, but that Native Americans discovered *him* on various beaches in the Caribbean. Long time Yale historian Sydney Ahlstrom wrote *A Religious History of the American People,*[59] but you must read one hundred fifty pages before finding – in a footnote – any mention of the Spanish mission in America that by 1560 planted a church in Pecos, New Mexico. That Spanish mission predates by sixty years the arrival of English Pilgrims and Puritans in New England. It predates by forty years the arrival of Anglicans in Virginia. That mission was planted during the lifetime of John Calvin in Geneva. When you live and teach at Yale,

---

[58] Mark A. Noll, *A History of Christianity in the United States and Canada* (Grand Rapids MI: Eerdmans, 1992), pp. 136-139.
[59] New Haven CT: Yale University Press, 1972.

or whatever place, you tend to launch history from your context and your kind of people.

Now we know for sure that a black church in Savannah, Georgia, with the support of slaves, slave churches, and slaves freed by the British occupation of Savannah, smuggled their two missionaries under cover of darkness to the river and sent them on their way. George Liele went to Jamaica to plant a church that ultimately created the Jamaican Baptist Convention. David George went first to Nova Scotia, and then on to Africa to plant churches, beginning in Liberia. They did this two decades before white New England Baptists got together to support the Judsons.

Many of you know that since 1977, Corean and I have been adoptive parents of an African American son, Brian, now a college graduate with military service, who at this writing is a social case worker with aging mentally, emotionally, and physically challenged adults. His son Jordan went to Bethune-Cookman University in Florida on a basketball scholarship, and graduated with honors as a business major. Now he is debating whether to play basketball professionally, or accept the offer to have his master's degree paid for if he would coach for his university.

Both have been on this trail. I am grateful to be able to say to them, as well as other African Americans who walk this trail, that the people who came in chains, who survived the passage and their chattel existence, were the first Americans who volunteered to get back on ships and cross oceans, to share God's grace and forgiveness with the people who never heard that old, old story of Jesus and his love. I have heard some people say that black Christians don't seem to be interested in missions. It is not true, but what missions did you ever know that recruited black missionaries? Allow me to share another true story.

In 1895 Moody Bible Institute graduated Mary McCloud from her one-year course. D. L. Moody had personally recruited her to come as a student. She then applied to the Presbyterian mission as a missionary to Africa, and was turned down because she was black. Imagine! You had to be white to be an evangelical missionary to black Africa! Discouraged, she went to Daytona Beach, Florida, and started a little school for black girls. Later she married Bethune. Later still, the Cookman boys college joined her girls college to become the alma mater of our grandson.

In 1935, Mary became a special assistant and advisor to President Franklin Roosevelt on education, and as a good friend of First Lady Eleanor Roosevelt, she influenced housing and justice reforms in Washington.[60]

Perhaps it was her unfortunate marriage and later divorce that hushed this story of arguably the most famous MBI graduate while we were students there from 1956-1959. She died in 1955. I am grateful that Joe Stowell, a former MBI president, had a plaque installed in her honor, near the D. L. Moody historical exhibit at Moody. As we say, *mas vale tarde que nunca.* "Better late than never."

---

[60] Nancy Ann Zrinyi Long, *The Life and Legacy of Mary McLeod Bethune* (Boston: Pearson Custom Publishing, 2006).

SHAFTESBURY OF ENGLAND

1801 to 1885

SHAFTESBURY OF ENGLAND

The story of William Wiberforce, William Pitt, and John Newton has become well known through the contemporary movie. Charles Simeon of Cambridge, Hannah More, and John Venn were also core members of that small group of evangelicals who met for fifty years in Clapham, to strategize for ways to stop the slave trade. It can be said that their little band of Wesleyan-influenced Anglicans spared England from a civil war, as they spent their lives and social capital confronting injustices in England, then the rapidly growing ruling power of the world. These Christians changed forever the previously accepted ideas that governments should only worry about wars, tariffs, and treaties, and, in Darwinian fashion, let social classes and structures become subservient to the survival of the fittest.

Anthony Ashley Cooper built on the progress of the Clapham group. Entering politics as the 7th Earl of Shaftesbury in 1926, as a conservative Tory with class and wealth to match, it was not long before his whole life moved toward a social concern for the poor and marginalized in England. It started when, as a young teen, he watched some drunks wheeling the body of a poor man to a paupers' open grave. The drunks laughed at the body as it bounced, then flopped into the street. In shock, the young lad made a vow that as an adult he would change the way the poor were buried in England. That vow came to fruition in 1849.

It took him ten years to get Parliament to pass the Ten Hours Bill, limiting work hours at a time when the Industrial Revolution was cranking up the Empire and labor was cheap. It took him another ten years to get

Parliament to pass a bill to widen mineshafts more than eighteen inches so adults, rather than children, could mine coal. Mining companies repeatedly complained that the added costs of wider shafts would hopelessly prevent them from competing with German coal. Frustrated, he hired an artist to sketch the pubescent and topless little boys and girls as they descended down the mineshafts, into the darkness where no adult could supervise. Not surprisingly, the Victorians responded when they saw the artist's etchings and voted to change the law.

When the children of poor families emerged from the mines, there were no schools for them to attend. He created the ragged school movement and started the first school in the western world where, at public expense, commoners' children could be educated. All students learned to read the King James Bible. His assumption: all should be able to read their own indictment when facing the Creator at the end time.

Like many Anglicans influenced by Wesley, he often went to prisons on Sunday to visit and speak to prisoners as Christ mentions in Matthew 25. He was horrified to find that not just paupers were routinely tossed into prison, but also the mentally challenged, the so called lunatics. In 1845 he persuaded Parliament to create a permanent Lunacy Commission, and remained its chair until his death forty years later.

He created the London water board, and for six years helped that board clean swamps and deliver potable water to Dickens' London, where typhus and cholera killed thousands. About that time, the British East India Company was setting up to rule India in Calcutta, in a swampy area adjacent to the Hughli River. I discovered, on my first of many visits to the cities of India, that the British installed London-style sewer systems. In Calcutta,

168

a unique system allowed the Hughli River to flow through city water pipes so that hundreds of thousands could bathe in water works influenced by Shaftsbury. He realized that chimneysweeps, young boys working above the oppressively smoky coal-burning fireplaces, continually faced hazards. In 1875 he got a new law passed that forbad the use of children to clean chimneys.

When he died in 1885, Queen Victoria sent word by telegraph to every train in England and every British ship on the seas to stop their engines for one minute in honor of the man who changed the world more than any man since Jesus Christ. Here is the surprise. His whole life was plagued by fits of anger, depression, and despondency. He loved Jesus but found it hard to love people, especially his political enemies. On occasion he would stop a speech in mid-sentence and disappear for weeks, only to reappear and continue where he left off.

When he visited prisons and saw the mentally ill, he realized that if he were poor and not privileged, he also would have been locked up. His biographer, Georginia Battiscombe, noticed that publicly he could put on a Victorian front, while privately his diaries were aflame with struggles. Her thesis: if he had been normal, he would not have found the tenacity to stay focused for decade after decade on single goals. He would have moved on to other agendas. I know now that the man who transformed the world was neither nice nor healthy, "yet no man has in fact ever done more to lessen the extent of human misery or to add to the sum total of human happiness."[61]

---

[61] Georgina Battiscombe, *Shaftesbury: The Great Reformer 1801-1885* (Boston: Houghton Mifflin Co., 1975), p. 344.

An English contemporary, John Nelson Darby (1800 to 1882) and a founder of the Plymouth Brethren, developed dispensational theology. Everyone who has a *Scofield Reference Bible* understands this perspective. Society is in a downward, sinful spiral. All reform is futile. Eventually Christians will be raptured out of the world. Reform will come when Christ returns. I have heard many preachers and teachers take Darby's side.

My view is that human sinfulness that becomes institutionalized in business and governmental structures makes reform difficult, but not impossible. US history confirms that Christians have been effective in bringing righteousness and justice to the public square. While in college I read Timothy Smith's *Revivalism and Social Reform*,[62] then Charles Foster's *Errand of Mercy*.[63] Later, I read Norris Magnusson's *Salvation in the Slums*[64] about how A. B. Simpson and others engaged in social reform long before it became a modernist or liberal agenda. If you are still not convinced that Evangelicals can impact societies and cultures, read *Saints in Politics*.[65]

I believe in the calling of the powerful to speak truth to power and advocate for justice until Christ comes or calls for us. We have many biblical texts that require that of us. I thank God for Wilberforce and Shaftesbury, two

---

[62] *Revivalism and Social Reform: In Mid-Nineteenth-Century America* (NY: Abingdon Press, 1957).

[63] *Errand of Mercy: The Evangelical United Front 1790-1837* (Chapel Hill NC: The University of North Carolina Press, 1960).

[64] *Salvation in the Slums: Evangelical Social Work, 1865-1920* (NJ: The Scarecrow Press, 1977).

[65] Ernest Marshall Howse, *Saints in Politics: The 'Clapham Sect' and the Growth of Freedom* (London: George Allen & Unwin LTD, 1973).

170

powerful saints in politics. Simultaneously with Shaftesbury, Charles Spurgeon pastored five thousand commoners at Metropolitan Tabernacle in central London. How many of them survived cholera or typhus, were able to read or have days off to hear great sermons? Very few I think. For me, parliament and pulpit are two sides of urban ministry.

TERESA OF INDIA

1910 to 1997

TERESA OF INDIA

Agnese Gonxhe Bojaxhiu was born in Albania. Her father died when she was a child. Her mother raised her Roman Catholic in a country that was predominately Orthodox at that time. At age twelve she knew she had a calling to ministry. At age eighteen she had hoped to leave directly for India, but was required by her order, the Sisters of Loreto, to do a postulant year as a test of her religious life. During that year in Ireland, she learned English. In 1929 she arrived in India to teach in the mountains at Darjeeling. When she took her vows in 1931 she chose the name Teresa, after a patron saint of missionaries. In 1937 she began teaching in Calcutta, but the overwhelming poverty of the poor challenged her to revise her plans. Wearing a sari of her own design – white with blue trim – she began helping the neediest she could find. In 1946, when India struggled to be liberated from the British, terrible riots between Hindus and Moslems made life much worse for millions. She appealed to the Vatican, and in 1950 was granted permission to begin a new order: Sisters of Charity, to care for the neglected, the hungry, the unloved, the shunned, the lepers, and the dying.

She found an abandoned Hindu Temple and turned it into the Kalighat Home for the Dying, a free hospice for the poor. I visited it five years ago. You almost need to fight your way through the crowds to get to the door. Her oft-repeated idea was that the people who live like animals should die like angels—loved and wanted. The Sisters founded leprosy clinics around the city, followed by ministry centers throughout the country. Today there are some five thousand Sisters working in about one hundred twenty countries.

There have been critics. Some Hindus have accused her of practicing secret baptisms for the dying. Others have commented that she treats the victims, but does nothing to challenge the evil systems that create gigantic social ills. I have read and also heard that the Marxist government, while respecting her, chided her for being dependent on western funding. Some critiqued her for medical malpractice, by not doing diagnosis, or by re-using needles and instruments. A few Sisters left the order, feeling that she was too dictatorial. I suppose there may be some truth in a few allegations, to which my borrowed response would be: "I like the way she is doing it better than the way I am not doing it."

Five years ago I heard a lecturer in Calcutta, now called Kolkata, tell us that Calcutta is a great blessing to the poor. "Imagine!" he said, "There are eighteen million people in this city and fifteen million are able to eat and survive on one dollar a day. No other city in the world can make that claim." I cannot help but feel that Hinduism, with its caste system that locks peoples into their existing conditions, has something to do with the spirit of resignation I sense when I am there.

By contrast, Christianity creates expectations. You do not *go* to temple. You *are* temple, indwelt by the Holy Spirit of the living God. Knowing this, Christians usually clean up the inside (spiritual transformation) and then go on to clean up environments. Christianity creates tensions in cultures with rigidly fixed social and vocational categories by giving rise to what I call the *inflation of expectations*. Marx called religion an opiate and some kinds of religions function that way. But while Christians are a minority in Kolkata, both Catholics and Evangelicals are doing amazing ministry: healing and teaching in clinics and schools all over the city.

In 1979 Teresa received the Nobel Peace Prize. She has been honored by most civilized nations. I was most struck by hearing her say: "I don't love the poor; I don't even know them, but when I see Jesus in them, to care for them is an act of worship." Her Matthew 25 theology, which resembles that of her hero Francis, transforms social work into worship. It is not about doing good. It is worship.

I heard Mother Teresa at a Presidential Prayer Breakfast in Washington D. C. during Bill Clinton's second term. When Vice President Al Gore's turn came to speak, he began by telling us how excited he was to be on the same platform with her. He was accustomed to power, but she was special. To tell how he felt that day, he told a true story. The Chicago Bulls had a rookie player who never got to play, but one night he got into a game, and scored one point, while his teammate, Michael Jordan, scored sixty-nine points. In the locker room after the game, the press gathered about the rookie to chide him about only scoring one point when Michael scored sixty-nine. Finally he said: "You guys have it all wrong. I will always remember this game as the night Michael Jordan and I combined for 70 points!" Our crowd roared, including me. We all got his point. The truth is that none of us belonged on the same platform with Mother Teresa.

She died about a week after the tragic death of Princess Diana, so some may not have noticed that the Hindu government of India gave her a state funeral. The Sisters still meet in their modest hall on Lower Circular Road, next to the Baptist church where I taught in 1981. Her tomb is on the first floor, and a sculpture of her in prayer sits on the second floor, around which the Sisters gather to pray before they spread all over the city helping the poor.

Teresa of Calcutta is without doubt the most famous urban ministry leader in my lifetime.

She also reminds me of a statistic I heard at a 1980 world mission event in Thailand. About seventy percent of all cross cultural and mission workers of the world are women. We men are a small minority of those serving Christ as ministers in cities. My thirty-five years in the inner city of Chicago showed me the strategic necessity for their involvement. In the most violent communities of all cities, gangs form and claim turf. All my studies and experience with gang literature confirmed that only women safely engage the gang culture of emasculated males, rendered powerless by absentee forces that most often control their communities. White males especially, are a perceived threat. Gangs can spot fear in us. Often, like bees and dogs that sense fear, they attack. Women ministers cut right through this fog of inner city war to do effective ministry. I told groups for years that if they have no plans to commission their sisters for inner city ministries, they prove they are not really serious about ministry there.

Thank you for walking the mission trail, a celebration of twenty centuries of faithful Christians crossing boundaries to share the good news of Jesus Christ around the world. This is the day that the Lord has made for you and me. Let us rejoice and be glad in it!

PART III: HOPE

One more theme permeates this story. Hope. Bakken is a testament to the hope that outlives us. Christopher Wright has written this summary:

> The whole Bible renders to us the story of God's mission, through God's people, in their engagement with God's world for the sake of the whole of God's creation.[66]

My Philadelphia friend, Tony Compolo, put it like this: "I read the last chapter. We win!"

Philosophically, I put myself in the category of realists. I am neither a pessimist nor an optimist. As a professor at Northern Baptist Theological Seminary in Chicago, I took my students all over that city. One of my favorite stops was Holy Angels Catholic Church, where Father George Clements would remind us that the way we change the ghetto is by education. Every parent of the one thousand students at Holy Angels' school was required to attend classes two nights a week to study what the kids were learning, so they could assist them. Then he said, "Change will come in the third generation." Real change is slow.

Nicodemus, the only person who ever heard Jesus say, "be born again," did not become a believer in Jesus' lifetime. Jesus was dead by the time Nicodemus identified himself

---

[66] Christopher Wright, *The Mission of God: Unlocking the Bible's Grand Narrative* (Downers Grove IL: InterVarsity Press, 2006), p. 51.

with the other followers. Salvation is switching Kingdoms.

I learned early on in Chicago that what we read in the paper or heard on television seldom included the signs of hope that I found, as I sought to fulfill my early vow to study Chicago. The Spirit was moving. Dr. Claude Marie Barbour – Parisian born scholar, former missionary in South Africa, and for several years my faculty colleague in an urban ministry course – believed the Holy Spirit was active in one of the worst crime areas in the city: Grand Boulevard and Oakland on the south side. This new white woman doctoral graduate began going around the dangerous streets asking in thick French accent, "Excuse me, but can you tell me what God is doing in this community?" Nobody laughed.

One day, someone responded by telling her that she must meet Hattie Williams on South Lake Park, a desolate street facing a housing project. Claude Marie knocked on the door and said, "Hattie, people in this community told me that God is speaking to you. May I move in with you and pay rent, while you teach me what God is teaching you?" So Dr. Barbour moved in to be the student of a divorced mother of six who was on public aid, but had received a vision for the community, and had written it down on a paper in her Bible. A couple years later, Claude Marie and I were bringing our students from Catholic Theological Union and Northern Baptist every week, for a team-taught seminar in Hattie's house, where she would lay hands on our students, and commission them for ministry.

When I received the call from the Lausanne Committee in 1979 that led to my twenty-year volunteer role as Senior Associate for Large Cities, I began yearlong studies of major cities that ended with consultations on six continents. The timing was right. A decade before, I had

178

done a post-master's degree at McCormick, where urban community studies were driven by the then popular research model that had the researcher doing *needs analysis* of poor neighborhoods. The study was designed to prove that we would be needed to solve those problems. All we had to do was find a foundation that would give us the money so we could provide the services to the poor.

Not long after that, I met John McKnight and Mary Nelson, Bill Leslie and Bud Ipema, and from our conversations a whole new paradigm emerged. Asset Based Community Development (ABCD) was born, and no one could articulate it better than John McKnight. By the time I entered and finished my own doctoral studies at McCormick, the theory and even the theology had changed. We no longer go looking for problems. We go searching for the signs of hope, and join them to see if we can partner and build their capacity. Hattie and Claude Marie gave me a vision of how that could be implemented in practice. What I came to see is that the basic assumption at the core of these ABCD's of urban ministry is the concept that there are "green shoots in the concrete." Development starts with hope.

My counsel to Lausanne and World Vision colleagues became simply this: Let's go find every bishop in the city and ask, "If you had to prove that God is alive in this city, what would you point to, to prove it?" Everyone has favorite ministry models. Our consultations were designed to bring those people together in a room with less than one hundred, to teach each other what they were doing and what they were learning in the city. It was not about me telling them what to do. I was the chief student in the process. It was Claude Marie's upside down model taken global. In more than two hundred cities people came together and shared. The week included at least one day when we got into buses or vans to explore what God was doing. In the process, Protestant Evangelicals met Catholics or Orthodox and everyone met the Pentecostals. In our reflection time we tried to put names on what we had seen and learned. In every case we saw reasons for hope and encouragement, especially to those church leaders who had almost no idea what the Body of Christ was doing in other denominations or in other parts of their city.

Twenty-five years ago I wrote an essay for what is still my all time favorite mission journal, *The International Bulletin of Missionary Research*, published by the Overseas Ministry Study Center in New Haven, Connecticut. In the October issue of 1984 I reported that eighty-five to ninety percent of the major barriers to urban ministry effectiveness were not in the cities at all, but inside the constricting churches or mission structures in which people tried to minister. I found that ministers could invent and describe solutions they knew would meet the spiritual and social needs of cities and city peoples, but when I asked why they did not implement their plans, they said things like:

> O my Board would never let me do that.
> My denomination would never help us fund that.
> My seminary never prepared me to do that.
> They'll call us liberal if we do that.

I had assumed that many pastors were discouraged and beaten down by their big bad city, and that what they needed from me was information and motivation. It turns out that most of the ministry solutions are accessible, and there are places where we can go or schools where we can study and learn what is working all over the world. Sadly, far too many of my colleagues give up hope when their church, denomination, or mission organizations become more oppressive to them than the world they are trying to serve.

For me there was no magic bullet. But I can testify that the small support group, that I met with monthly for the last twenty-eight years I was in Chicago, provided the realistic encouragement I came to know as *hope under pressure*. I also learned to drink deeply at the well of mission history, where I saw that people could take the basic core of biblical truth and down load it into multiple contexts. I saw that, whereas my work might be shrinking and results diminishing, the Kingdom of God was exploding in the global south of Asia, Africa and Latin America. I saw my world as part of a much larger drama. That perspective helped give me hope and courage to be faithful when not successful.

At Bakken we observe the church year which begins with Advent, a season of expectation. It comes at the time of the year when we transition to eighteen hours of darkness in this community just south of the Canadian border. Near the darkest day of the year we remember the birth of our Lord, and when Easter comes, we remember that one grave is empty. We live by what the Bible calls the *blessed hope*.

The more than two thousand trees I have planted at Bakken will not mature even in our sons' lifetimes. To plant a tree is a commitment to the future. We are not naïve. Wars, fires, earthquakes, accidents, sickness and ultimately our deaths are part of life, but they are not the endgame for us. When doubts and discouragement come, I plant more trees. The flowers that push their way through the winter snows at Bakken remind us that we are part of God's mission and a Kingdom that lasts forever.

So I return to the major themes I mentioned at the beginning of this book: grace, Trinity, family, community, church, books, trees, celebration, and Gospel. It turns out that hope is the way we integrate these themes and practice our faith on a daily basis. We have come full circle from Saxon to Chicago and back.

Allow me to close this reflection with a benediction that has become a Bakken tradition.

> To God be the glory,
> and to the earth be peace;
> to the Christians be courage,
> and to our world be hope.
> Amen!

PART IV: BIBLIOGRAPHICAL ESSAY

I beg your patience while I share briefly about my own journey in the historical field. An old friend, Ted Ward, told me thirty years ago that eventually people would be more interested in how I learn, rather than in what I know. I have been a ministry practitioner for fifty years. This year is the anniversary of my entry into a Seattle church in 1959 as assistant to the pastor. Simultaneously I entered Seattle Pacific College (now university) as a history major to complete my bachelor's degree. History is not just a study of the past, but a study of the written record of the past. Historiography was a senior seminar for history majors where we seriously analyzed the social locations and biases of the writers of history.

My course in 1965 with Dr. Roy Swanstrom was one of the most influential courses I ever experienced. My professor in several courses and also my advisor, he modeled a way to integrate his Ph.D. studies at Berkley with his Swedish Covenant pietism. Our third child arrived as a stillborn during that seminar, in the final month before my graduation. He helped pastor me, interceded with other professors to alter my final exam schedules, then remained an encouraging friend until his death more than twenty-five years later.

I learned shortly, however, that my calling was not to be in the trenches of historical scholarship, but in trying to make sense of it for those like myself, on the mission journey in a world shifting from rural to urban, where the nations now resided in the neighborhoods of my parishes. Permit me to share an overview of how the discipline of Christian history has changed in my lifetime. In so doing, I will share some texts that provided background for the mission trail at Bakken. Organizing for the trail, back in 1995, provided reflection time on how history had been changing.

First, I reviewed the standard church history text I used in seminary: *A History of the Christian Church*, by Williston Walker.[67] The problem with this book, and many others like it, is that it focused on the center of church life, what we might call the three C's: canon, creeds and church organizations. Little attention was given to what went on around the edges of the Roman Empire, and later the Holy Roman Empire. I have come to call it *a telephone directory of the past.* This approach compresses data, takes all the fun out of history, and marginalizes the mission of the church. Those were the days when professors assigned readings in dense studies such as the *History of Dogma* in seven volumes by Adolph Harnack.[68]

That is when I began to realize that some of the best missionaries were locked out of official Christendom essentially because they lost the vote in the councils that made the creeds. One of my favorites was Ulfilas, the Arian, who, when forced to leave the Roman Empire, went to the war-making Gothic tribes. He translated the Bible but left out the books of Kings because "he decided the Goths already knew enough about war." You can find that in a footnote in Stephen Neill's *A History of Christian Missions.*[69] Ulfilas made a front line mission decision. He abbreviated the Bible for his context. So I ask, What

---

[67] Revised by Cyril Richardson, Wilhelm Pauck, and Robert Handy (NY: Charles Scribner's Sons, 1959).
[68] Tran. from the 3rd German edition by Neil Buchanan (NY: Dover Publications, Inc., 1961).
[69] (Baltimore MD: Penguin Books, 1964), p. 55.

preacher among us has not avoided the tough texts of Scripture lest we offend our congregations?

Second, I was fortunate early on to access Kenneth Scott Latourette and his seven volume set as an alternative way to view history: *A History of the Expansion of Christianity*.[70] A layman born in China, Latourette's focus on expansion led him to feature the church crossing cultures. He was at his best in the volumes when he describes "the impact of the church on cultures followed by the impact of the cultures on the church." His Yale colleague Roland Bainton wrote *Christendom: A Short History of Christianity and Its Impact on Western Civilizatiion* in two volumes.[71] As you can tell from the title, his focus is on the changes to societies brought about by the church, but the focus is still intentionally western civilization. Baintain is less wordy than Latourette, and a masterful storyteller whose books read like the lectures I heard and still remember a half-century later.

Third, I consulted the specific mission histories, especially my two-dollar, twenty-five-cent original Pelican edition of Stephen Neill's, *A History of Christian Missions*.[72] Neill was a New Testament scholar at Cambridge who became a long time missionary in India, and eventually authored a three volume set on the Christian history of India. I had the privilege of hearing him lecture. Like Bainton, he made me want to learn more, because he could talk about the significance of mission with interpretations based on marvelously descriptive case studies. Neill and Latourette are worth reading for their interpretative footnotes.

---

[70] CEP Ed. (Grand Rapids MI: Zondervanw 1970).
[71] NY: Harper & Row, 1964.
[72] Baltimore MD: Penguin Books: 1964.

But there is a problem with Neill. Women were absent in his narrative. That fact got rectified by a scholar I know and greatly admire, Ruth Tucker, who wrote *From Jerusalem to Irian Jaya: A Biographical History of Christian Missions.*[73] After reading it, I invited her to come for a public lectureship at Northern Seminary where I was teaching. But I also realized that over eighty percent of this five hundred-page work is given to missionaries in the past two centuries. I had to go elsewhere to get the earlier stories.

Francis M. DuBose, a dear man I had the privilege of knowing as the resident urbanologist at Golden Gate Seminary near San Francisco, wrote helpful summary introductions to nearly all the missionaries I chose for the mission trail in his *Classics of Christian Mission.*[74] Manschreck and Bettenson produced helpful historical document books, but DuBose is focused on mission documents.

Fourth, I explored Catholic writers, since most of the mission history on the trail is Catholic and Orthodox. Now I make a confession. When I was a student at Moody Bible Institute, I saw an ad on the subway for a free correspondence course offered by the Paulist Fathers. It was 1957 and I was beginning to feel that my classroom instruction might not be the whole story. Soon I received my 85-cent new, but now falling apart, copy of *A Popular History of the Catholic Church* by Philip Hughes[75] and sent my weekly exams by mail. Short answers to my questions promptly arrived from Father Fitzgerald, who usually suggested that I consult *The Catholic*

---

[73] Grand Rapids MI: Academie Books, 1983.
[74] Francis M. DeBose, ed (Nashville TN: Broadman Press, 1979).
[75] Garden City NY: Doubleday, 1956.

Encyclopedia. It proved to be a counter-point to what I was studying at Moody, especially the Reformation, called *The Protestant Revolt.* I learned early that bias and perspective are always part of history.

The year I began teaching at Northern Baptist Seminary, an English Catholic scholar, Paul Johnson, wrote *A History of Christianity.*[76] It remains the best single volume I have read. I revisited him while working on the mission trail.

Fifth, I began to read histories that went beyond the traditional western perspective. The first of these was *The Story of Christianity* in two volumes by Justo Gonzales.[77] I used and very much enjoyed his three volume *A History of Christian Thought*[78] in my part-time adjunct teaching at McCormick Seminary (1969-1977). I was pastoring in a neighborhood that was becoming Puerto Rican and I had joined the board of Latin America Mission. That required a plunge into all things Latin, including broadening my perspective on the Catholic missions, which this Methodist scholar from the Caribbean did very well indeed.

Over the years I had been reading essays, and occasionally heard Andrew Walls bring a new perspective on the writing of African and European Christianity. Finally, his book of collected essays appeared in 1996: *The Missionary Movement in Christian History: Studies in the Transmission of Faith.*[79]

The writing of Christian history has become global. My first book from this perspective, edited by English

---

[76] NY: Atheneum, 1979.
[77] HarperSanFrancisco, 1984.
[78] Nashville TN: Abingdon Press, 1970.
[79] Maryknoll NY: Orbis Books.

historian, Adrian Hastings, was *A World History of Christianity*.[80] The year we moved from Chicago to Bakken, David Chidester, a history professor from South Africa, wrote *Christianity, A Global History*.[81] That was followed by the first of two volumes by Dale Irwin and Scott Sundquist: *History of the World Christian Movement*.[82] Two popular historical perspectives on world Christianity in this last decade, that I highly recommend, include *The Next Christendom: The Coming of World Christianity*, by Phillip Jenkins,[83] and *Disciples of All Nations: Pillars of World Christianity* by Lamin Sanneh.[84]

If it had not been clear before, it is now. From 1900 to 2000 the Christian church went from being eighty percent white to being more than fifty percent non-white; from being most populous in Europe and North America to dramatic growth in Latin America, Africa, and Asia. Latourette labeled the nineteenth century *the great century*, but today's historians can seriously question that. It is clear today that Christianity is now a non-western religion, as it was for the first thousand years, until the late conversions of Europe and North America.

I am assuming that graduate students who walk this trail realize there are period studies and contextual studies, many of which I have in my library, and which can be accessed by anyone who chooses, but those are details beyond the scope of this overview.

---

[80] Grand Rapids MI: Eerdmans, 1999.
[81] HarperSanFrancisco, 2000.
[82] Maryknoll NY: Orbis Books, 2001.
[83] NY: Oxford University Press, 2002.
[84] NY: Oxford University Press, 2008.

F——irst, let me describe the dictionaries and encyclopedias I used that provided brief backgrounds and useful summaries of every person on the trail. Most helpful to me, from the international perspective, was *The Oxford Dictionary of the Christian Church*, edited by F.L. Cross.[85] Equally useful, written a generation later, was *The New International Dictionary of the Christian Church*, edited by J.D. Douglas.[86] *The Dictionary of Christianity in America*, edited by Daniel Reid,[87] focuses primarily on mission to and from America. It goes beyond the *Handbook to Christianity in America*, edited by Mark Noll and others,[88] in which I contributed one article.

We are fortunate today for *A Dictionary of Asian Christianity*, edited by Scott Sundquist.[89] I used Samuel Hugh Moffett's first two of three volumes: *A History of Christianity in Asia.*[90] I especially prize the first volume because he sent me a kind note with a first edition gift copy. His wife Eileen and I served together on the Latin America Mission Board.

I will confess that when I came to Mother Teresa, I had two handicaps: first, she is a contemporary so is not

---

[85] NY: Oxford University Press, 1958.
[86] Grand Rapids MI: Zondervan, 1978.
[87] Downers Grove IL: InterVarsity Press, 1990
[88] Grand Rapids MI: Eerdmans, 1984.
[89] Grand Rapids MI: Eerdmans, 2001.
[90] Vol. 1: HarperSanFrancisco, 1992; Vol. 2: Maryknoll NY: 2006.

mentioned in most of my historical books; but also, I have only one serious book about her: *Teresa of Calcutta: A Pencil in God's Hand*, by Franca Zambonini.[91] It is a good introduction and cites other books, but is a biographical portrait rather than a reflective historical portrait. I did what I find all my students do under such circumstances: I googled *Wikipedia*, the free encyclopedia, and found that almost three million people have visited and added to information available there. While I know my history professors would frown on this, were I beginning my trail plans today, I could be tempted to search electronically for what exists beyond the nearly ninety-five hundred cataloged books in my library at Bakken. Truth be known, I am a relic of the past, a slave to books. I'm history!

The World Christian Encyclopedia by David Barrett[92] can provide me the latest status report on Christian mission for any country in the world. When, for example, I prepared the brief essay on Mother Teresa and wanted to see how many Catholic and Orthodox Christians there were in Albania in the decade before she was born, I found the percentages and tables. That led me to observe that Teresa's mother raised her in the minority Catholic religion. In 1900 the Orthodox were a much larger group. Both fell on hard times after the Russian Communist Revolution, which happened when she was seven years old. Albanian Christianity in 2009 is growing again. Imagine the surprise and delight of discouraged Catholics who died, and in heaven discovered that one of their own daughters was changing the churches and the world from a base in Calcutta!

---

[91] Tran. Jordan Aumann (NY: Alba House, 1993).

[92] Vol. I, 2nd edition (NY: Oxford University Press, 2001).

When I travel, I make copies of the country essays where I will be visiting. I started this when the first edition of *The World Christian Encyclopedia* came out in 1982, the year I began traveling in my role as Lausanne Associate for Large Cities. I found those historical, bibliographical, and statistical summaries incredibly helpful in my travels.

Perhaps I should close this brief essay on the trail resources with a challenge for you – the reader. If you find a great book or essay on any one of the twenty mission saints, please inform me at rayb@bgu.edu. I will be grateful first for the information, but also because I know you made it all the way through these academic notes at the end.

ACKNOWLEDGEMENTS

Once again I begin by giving thanks to God for showing marvelous kindness to me, and for the existence of this place we call Bakken. It has come about as divine choreography.

Thank you Aunt Ruth Bakke and Cousin Sandy Riley for first finding this place and then negotiating all the paper work that made the purchase possible. Thank you Cousin Gordon for answering numerous early morning phone calls from Chicago regarding projects such as clearing brush, cutting maple trees that paid for the power and phone lines, supervising construction of the cabin, arranging for the drilling of the well, watching over these acres in the eight years of our infrequent visits before final relocation here in 2000, and for bringing many gifts of plants and flowers.

My thanks to Roy Johnson who freely donated his D Six Cat and many hours to clearing, logging, and road building. He did all that, as he said, "for old times sake."

Thanks also go to Jim Hill of Mt. Vernon who built the wash house, the pump house, deck, and with a few kids under court supervision to whom he was teaching carpentry skills, built Fort Saxon, the children's play house in Amber's Village.

Thanks to Stephen Kollmar for helping Corean build two bat houses, and for his design of the rugged swing set at Amber's Village, and to Laura Kollmar for assisting Corean regarding decisions in the house.

Tom and John Latimer, from their home on the Mosquito Lake Road, installed a complex water system, built the wood shed, the gardening shed, and the swing set. They have the indispensable gift of knowing how to make repairs, and a willingness to let me call them when things break or quit functioning.

Our architect Pat Mitchell and builder Mark Gallatin combined to design and build the art piece that functions as our home, offices, and an inviting space for the many hundreds of people who come every year for vespers, concerts, occasional retreats, committee and board meetings.

John LaMonte was an early mentor and the first to volunteer a tool, pipe, or equipment when needed. He and Cousin Kit made the Bakke farm, three miles east at Saxon, into a special place with camp sites, cabin, and restored farm house, where family and church groups come to camp, and where many Bakken guests sleep over night.

Steve and Jacki Rossing own the historic Acme General Store. I thank them for a thousand acts of kindness shown us, and nearly everyone else in this community.

Special thanks to Bob Baker – the esteemed ex-marine, school bus driver, and now mayor of Acme – for conversations over thousands of cups of coffee at the store at 6 am, for checking up on me when I am away, and for helping Corean in emergencies.

Thanks also to Brad Smith, president of Bakke Graduate University (BGU) in Seattle, where I serve as chancellor and professor, who, with the Board of Directors, approved my summer long sabbatical, giving me time and space to write this book.

Carol Quinton of Van Zandt is my incomparable administrative assistant. She manages all the details of an internationally complex ministry by scheduling my

196

calendar, and helps to coordinate the BGU international Board of Regents and scholarship programs. She gives time to catalogue additions to my ever expanding library, and during this sabbatical handles my phone calls, emails, and correspondence.

Over the years, Joyce Ambrose and her late husband, Lawrence, allowed me to come to their Wickersham place and remove hundreds of little fir trees that I learned would grow well if planted in sunny areas. Walk a few yards down one of my tractor roads, just east of the Trinity Tree, and you will come to *Ambrose Woods*.

Rick Harkness has delivered countless loads of pit run gravel from his farm for making new roads and repairing old ones. Previously he excavated, put in culverts and trenches for water and power lines, and when the road washed out, returned to make it better than ever.

Judy and Al Reed moved back to Acme, to the Rothenbuhler farm of her father. Several times a year we reserve her five guests rooms and swimming pool, so that our many visitors can enjoy "World Class Acme."

My siblings – Marilyn, Dennis, and Lowell – have been all over these trails, encouraging our dreams and life style commitments. They have joined me in the ministry of Bakke Graduate University in scholarship development, board, and staff positions.

Don Dewey of Puyallup, a Boeing engineer turned farmer, taught me what I had long since forgotten, or never knew, about tractors. He helped me choose a John Deere 4500 and negotiated the deal with his good friend at Sumner Tractor. Seven hundred tractor hours and many tractor roads later, I say, Thanks, Don. At first Corean thought my tractor was the toy that would compensate for her concert piano, but now she knows better.

Dr. Bill O'Brien has been with me on this journey for more than twenty years. After serving as a music missionary in Indonesia and as a denominational mission executive, he and his late wife, Dellanna, took on mission assignments in Birmingham, Alabama. Bill and I collaborated on three citywide consultations in Birmingham while he taught at Beeson Divinity School of Sanford University. When my board formed BGU, I asked Bill to serve with me on the Board of Regents and on our faculty. When the Tsunami hit Banda Aceh, Indonesia, instantly killing some eighty thousand people, he persuaded the mayor and leaders of Frisco, Texas, to adopt that Muslim city as a sister city. He returns often to Indonesia to assist in many ways. Three years ago we team-taught a seminar there. As Corean can testify, I have no closer mission friend in the world than Bill, and I count it a great honor to have him write the foreword for this book.

Finally, I want to thank Woody and Andrea, Amber and Elijah, who have made Bakken their second home. Our son, Woody, a former paramedic and now a work based learning coordinator for special needs students at Oak Harbor High School, comes to spend weekends a couple times each month. With strength, tenacity, and vision, he has helped me turn steep, brushy hills into state park quality vistas with trails. He drew the maps and woodland illustrations for this book.

Andrea and Corean created a little company, Bakken Books, adapting the mission statement of Bakken for their identity as a publisher: "Committed to beauty, peace, and transformation." After watching them do their exacting work, I can say without fear of contradiction, that writing my draft was the easy part.

God's peace and my thanks to all,

Ray Bakke

198